PRE-ROLL - 1980-1981

S.O.A

BLACK FLAG

Choice

PHILADELPHIA

JULY

THE STARLIGHT

UNWELCOMED SONGS

HENRY ROLLINS

Hey Ross,

Have A Good Read.

Henry Rollins

11-19-02

2.13.61
P.O. BOX 1910 · LOS ANGELES ·
CALIFORNIA · 90078 · USA

COPYRIGHT

Design: Chapple Design

ISBN: 1-880985-71-3

2.13.61 Publications
P.O. Box 1910
Los Angeles, CA 90078
(800) 992-1361
(323) 969-8791
www.21361.com
www.henryrollins.com

ACKNOWLEDGEMENTS

Thanks: Carol Bua @ 2.13.61,
Dave Chapple, Mitch Bury of Adams Mass.

Special thanks to all those who came through with great photos. Thanks for being there at the time and making the effort to document the moment.

Inspiration: Greg Ginn, Ian MacKaye, Guy Picciotto, Iggy Pop, Alan Vega, Mark E. Smith, Nick Cave, Roky Erickson, and the countless other great songwriters to which so many of us owe a great debt.

Joe Cole 4.10.61 — 12.19.91

TABLE OF CONTENTS

CHAPTER 1: PRE-ROLL

PAGE 3

CHAPTER 2: 1981-1986

PAGE 19

CHAPTER 3: 1986

PAGE 47

CHAPTER 4: 1987

PAGE 57

CHAPTER 5: 1988-1989

PAGE 87

CHAPTER 6: WARTIME

PAGE 133

CHAPTER 7: 1990-1992

PAGE 143

CREDITS

PAGE 197

CHAPTER 1: PRE-ROLL

The Extorts. L to R: Wendel, Simon, Lyle, Mike

I spent the first twenty years of my life in Washington DC. I think the most relevant event in those years for me was the arrival of punk rock. In my early teens, I saw a few arena bands like Led Zeppelin, Ted Nugent, Aerosmith and Van Halen. It was great but I always felt so far away from the music.

In the late seventies people I knew were forming bands and getting gigs. I went to as many gigs and practice sessions as I could. Countless afternoons I spent in Nathan Strejcek's basement watching the Teen Idles practice. Their practice was as good as their gigs. Years later, it occurred to me how lucky I was to have seen them so many times. This time period was a complete turning point for me. All of a sudden, the music was right in my face. I met the bands. I made friends. I sort of fit in. The impact of all this I have never quite recovered from. ✶ ✶ ✶

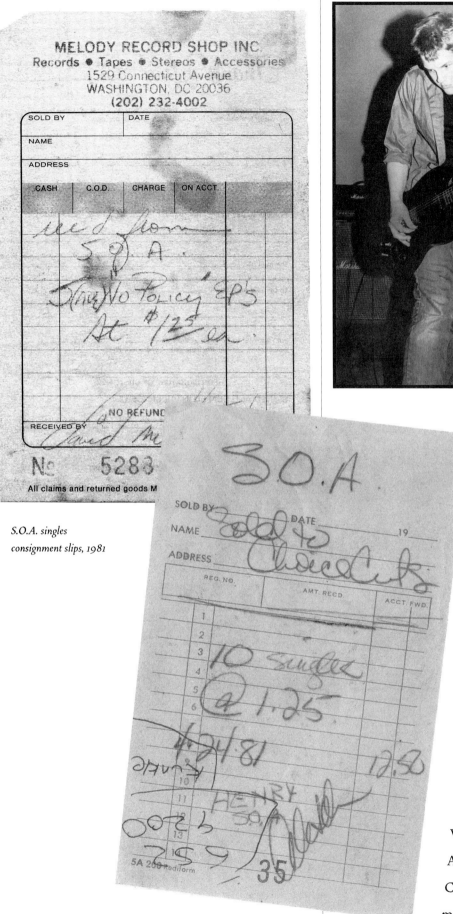

Mike Hampton

*S.O.A. singles
consignment slips, 1981*

Music had changed. There were bands that as far as I was concerned, were making the music I had been waiting all my life to hear. The Buzzcocks, The Ramones, The Damned, The UK Subs, The Lurkers, The Clash, Generation X, The Ruts, X Ray Spex, Sham 69, Suicide, The Cramps, 999, Devo, Eater. Bands who made one or two singles and slipped into history like The Valves, The Panik, The Skunks, Art Attacks, Pure Hell, The Cigarettes, The Killjoys and so many more. These were some of

Wendel Blow

In the middle of all this revelation and blur, Lyle Presslar vacated the vocalist slot in the Extorts to join some band called Minor Threat as their guitar player. I joined the singerless band. I had no experience of course. All of a sudden I have lyrics to write, band practice to go to, arguments to have, all that cool stuff.

We were a band. We had a name. State of Alert. We were Henry on vocals, Mike on guitar, Wendel on bass and Simon on drums. We were not very good. Mike was though, and really turned into something special as a guitarist and songwriter in years to come in bands like Faith, Embrace and Manifesto. I had never really written lyrics before.

the early singles I was checking out. As the years went by, many more would come.

The record store became an ever increasingly visited place for us all. Probably the one most occupied and plundered was Yesterday and Today, located at 1327 J Rockville Pike in Rockville MD. The man most hounded was its owner Skip Groff. We were there all the time. We must have driven Skip nuts. It was Skip who helped some of us make our early records. Skip produced SOA's single. He remains a friend to this day and I still visit the store when I can. He's been one of the great constants in my life. I go all around the world and then walk into Y&T and there's Skip. He's one of the great ones. I always wanted to have one of our records go gold only so I could give one to Skip and see it on his wall.

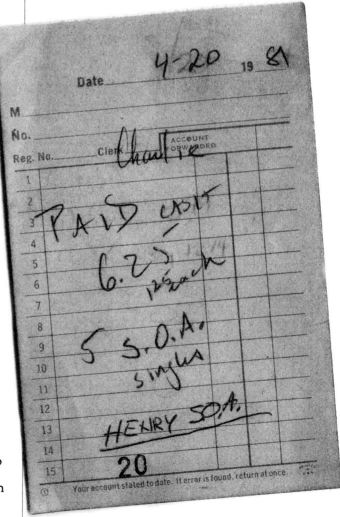

Henry and Skip Groff at Yesterday and Today Record Store, 2000

I just put down how I felt. We existed for several months, played a few shows and thanks to Skip, Don Zientera and his Inner Ear studios, and Ian and Jeff at Dischord, made a record.

At the time I was listening constantly to The Adverts, whose great songwriter, TV Smith, wrote some of the best lyrics I have ever heard. Check songs of his like Television's Over, My Place, Back from the Dead, Safety in Numbers. To this day, TV continues to write brilliant songs. If you read the lyrics that people like Ian MacKaye and other DC music scene types were writing and take into account the great records I was listening to at the time, you would think that some of it would have rubbed off on me. I guess it didn't rub hard enough.

Besides our own great local scene with bands like the Bad Brains, Minor Threat, The Untouchables, The Enzymes, Trench Mouth, Black Market Baby and others, out-of-towners Black Flag's Nervous Breakdown and Jealous

Again EPs had an immediate and profound impact on me. Ginn and Dukowski were masters of capturing the moment. Songs that were 100% committed. The kind of emotional intensity that is so honest and crushing, an honesty that you almost want to apologize for because of the damage it could possibly do to someone who wasn't prepared for it. That's what I wanted to hear. Songs that were strong enough to blast away the tonnage of life's oppressive grind. This, coupled with an equally physical delivery is the ultimate combination. It's obviously not everyone's particular favorite way to go but so be it. Below are a few songs from those days. The first one, Go North, I wrote for Ian MacKaye's first band, The Slinkees.

S.O.A, DC, 1980

Go North young man!
go go north, north, North
higher, higher
Past New ENgland
Past Canada
Go to Alaska
Artificial Preservatives NO!
Crime + Deceit + lies NO!
Polution, war, Famine NO!
Cancer, Nuclear melt downs NO! NO! NO!
Simple life and death
air, sun, water, cold
The reality is so sharp it will
cut you like a knife
You can't lie, or pretend to
be something you're not, because No one
will hear you.
It's cold because it is
It's dark because it is
It's true becaus it is
No microwave ovens in alaska.

Go North original lyric sheet, 1979

Minor Threat show, DC, 1980

LOST IN SPACE

Up in smoke

I laugh in your face

Fucked up on drugs

Lost in space

See your friends

They laugh at you

But don't get mad

They're fucked up too

Spend your time on the floor

Go throw up

Go back for more

Eat those pills take those thrills

Who's gonna wind up dead

—you

Snort that coke what a joke

Who's gonna wind up dead

—you

SOA EXPENSES

PAID BY

H	DRUM'S	40.00
H	FLIERS	4.20
H	FLIERS	21.20
H	FLIERS	18.56
H	SNARE HEAD	8.00
H	FIRST DEMO	76.50
H	CYMBALS	18.00
H	STAND + CYMBAL	30.00

$$216.46$$
$$- 95.00 \quad \text{DC SPACE} + 9:30$$
$$121.46$$

H	FIRST NIGHT	2̶8̶0.00
H	SECOND NIGHT	105.00
H	FINAL MIX	50.00

$$175.00$$

H	TEST PRESS + MASTERING	200.00

TOT 375.00

375.00
121.46
TOT 496.46

550
175
100
825

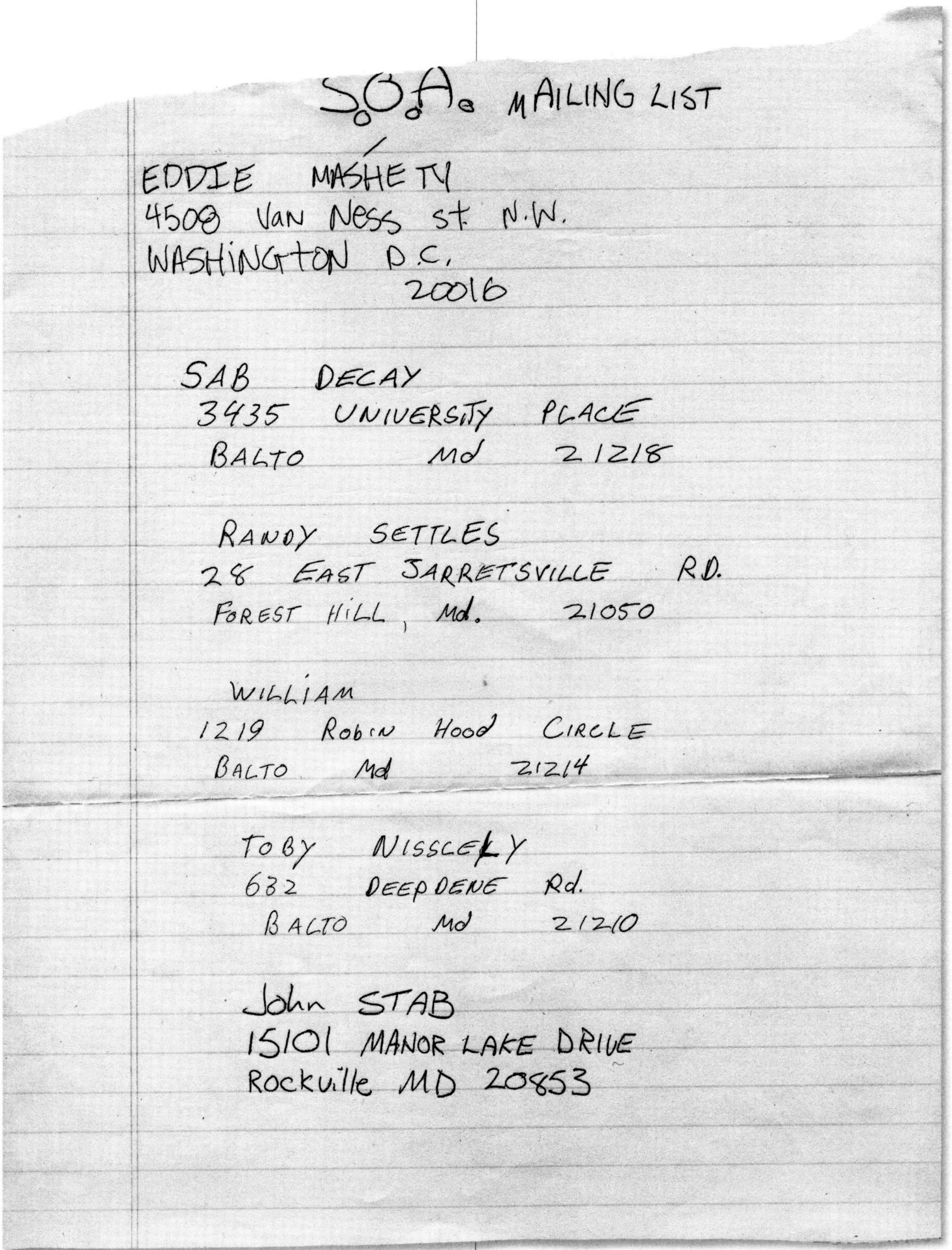

S.O.A. MAILING LIST

EDDIE MASHETY
4508 VAN NESS St. N.W.
WASHINGTON D.C.
20016

SAB DECAY
3435 UNIVERSITY PLACE
BALTO MD 21218

RANDY SETTLES
28 EAST JARRETSVILLE RD.
FOREST HILL, Md. 21050

WILLIAM
1219 ROBIN HOOD CIRCLE
BALTO MD 21214

TOBY NISSCELY
632 DEEP DENE Rd.
BALTO MD 21210

John STAB
15101 MANOR LAKE DRIVE
Rockville MD 20853

DRAW BLANK

Always ask me how I feel

You think that truth

is part of the deal

You'll never know

I'll never show

I'm not a book

You can't read me

Always ask me what's on my mind

I'll just tell you that I don't

have time

GIRL PROBLEMS

Call her on the phone

Oh shit, she isn't home

And you never know

She's not with someone else

Gotta say the right thing

She might think you're a fool

Gotta lie through your teeth

To make her think you're cool

I don't need girl problems

I've got troubles as it is

I don't need to waste my time

I don't need more shit

You lower your pride

Because you think she's what you need

So you don't mind the pain

Or the way you always feel

It's just a game

She's got you on a line

Throw your feelings to the wind

She's playing with your mind

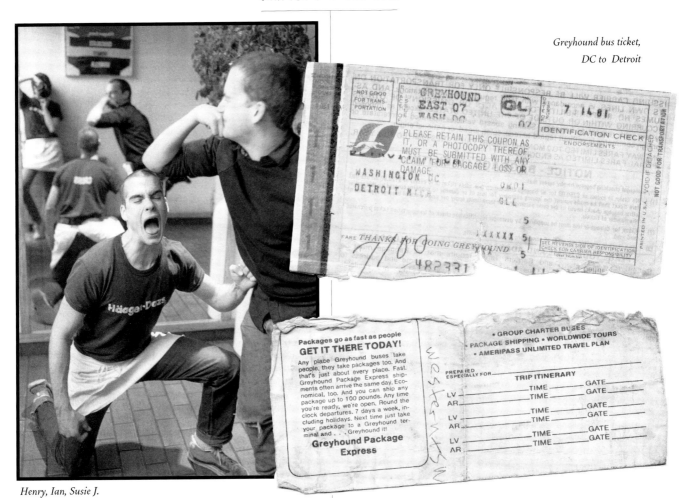

Greyhound bus ticket,
DC to Detroit

Henry, Ian, Susie J.

At the time, I was working at a Haagen Daz ice cream outlet. There wasn't much to this job skillwise, but it paid the rent. In the summer of 1981 I left the job and my hometown via Greyhound Bus to join Black Flag. I met up with them mid-tour in Detroit and have been touring and making records ever since.

John Chumbris, Susan Board, Henry

S.O.A, DC Space. Eddie Janney, center with back to camera.

It was quite an adjustment to make, going from a regular job to this new one. There were some bumps in the road as you might expect. Looking back at the whole thing, I think it was the right choice. I sometimes miss the streets of the city I grew up in. For over two decades now, I have traveled and lived all over the world. At this point, it's all I know. Home, if I have one, is the road.

CHAPTER 2: 1981-1986

CHAPTER 2: 1981-1986

Black Flag, London UK, 1981

It was on the Black Flag album My War and onwards that I got to add some lyrics to the Black Flag songlist. Previously, we had been playing all the songs that had been written before my arrival. Greg Ginn was the band's primary songwriter but was open to letting me have some lyrics in the mix. Whenever I told him I had a lyric idea, he told me to just bring him the words and he would come up with something. ✶✶✶

Black Flag, London UK, 1981

Sometimes he would have a song that he had no words for and he would let me have a crack at it. He was very cool about all this. That was the case

Black Flag, 100 club, London. Ian MacKaye on left

with the song that became Wound Up. Greg had left it unfinished as an instrumental and I asked him if I could put some words on it. I did the vocals on a version of the song that was done during the My War sessions first and then later for the album version. Black Flag recorded a lot. Greg was writing songs like there was no tomorrow. We found ourselves in the studio often. Early on, Spot, who had produced the early work of the band, was still at helm and I would do most of my vocals with him. Later on when Greg started producing, I would do my vocals with him. We did vocals quickly, usually in a few takes if that. Often, it was more about intensity than hitting all the notes. I know, what notes. Spot and I often worked late at night at a studio called Total Access in Hermosa Beach CA.

Black Flag, 100 Club, London, 1981

A lot of the Black Flag stuff was done there.

To keep things interesting, Spot and I would set up the mic in different places in the studio.

Black Flag NYC, December 1981.

One night we set up in the reception area and turned off all the lights. On some of the songs on side two of the My War album, you can hear furniture getting knocked over, the Coke machine groaning and empty water bottles hitting the wall. We were starting some of these sessions at one in the morning, studio time was cheaper then. We were just trying to stay awake. I will never forget those surreal walks back to SST with the din of

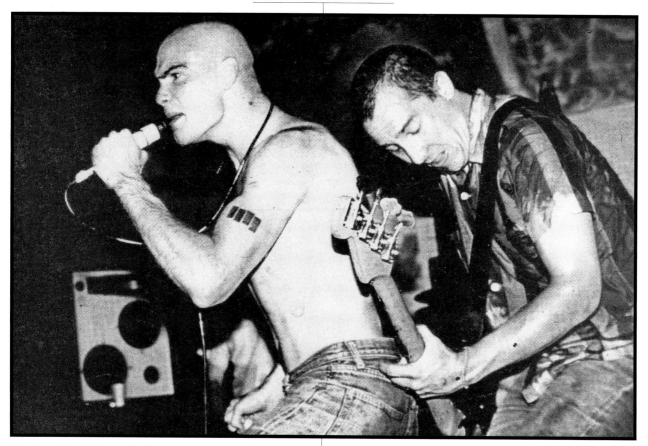

Huntington Beach, CA 1981 (both)

morning rush hour traffic filling my ears having
been up all night in the darkness of Total Access.

To this day I am amazed at the sheer volume of
Ginn's output in those days. There seemed no
stopping the guy. Anyway, here's my slim offerings
to the mighty Black Flag songbook.

DC, 1981

Wound Up

I walked by your house
To see if you were home
It was my only chance
I felt so all alone
It always seems I get so wound up
To feel so let down

Don't you ever see the way I look at you
Could you understand why I feel the
way I do

I have a lot to show you
I feel I have something to prove

There's things I'd like to tell you
But my brain is slow to move
I wish you would give me a second
So I could make you see
No one can look at you
And see the things I see

I have strong emotions
I keep them to myself
I know I can write them
I know I can sing them
That's what I'll have to do
Deep in my heart
I keep a picture of you

Los Angeles, 1982

San Francisco, 1982

WORKING NOTES: Nights spent alone in the room thinking of you. Never daring to tell you what was inside. I can get close. I can look and listen and watch you walk away with someone else. It hurts to watch. It brings me pain to think that you're out there and I'm alone here. If I told you my thoughts you might laugh in my face, leave me standing steeped in humiliation. That would make me want to die. Doesn't matter. A lot of things make me want to die. The silence in my room at night. The emptiness I feel at the end of the day when I walk home. The cold in my hands by the time I reach the door. All the time I spend thinking of you. You're out there somewhere laughing. The lights are warm and some cardboard man is with you. You will never know me.

Forever Time

```
Time
Forever time
It's time to walk by me one last
time
It's time
At first, relax, get set
Get your message from time

It's time to look into my eyes one
last time
It's time
I feel like some kind of death
machine
With skin  and muscle
And a heart that pumps my blood

It's time to kiss me goodbye one
last time
This is the first time
This is my last time
It's my only time
But it's only time
```

Swinging Man

Swinging man

Hanging around

I'm a swinging man

My feet never touch the ground

I go back and fourth

Looking for a little warmth

But I didn't find nothing

So I'm hanging around

Feeling no pain

All the girls know my name

I go by swinging man

I tell you what

You get yourself together and

you go downtown

And when you come home

I'll still be hanging around

I am the swinging man

And my feet never touch the ground

WORKING NOTES: I'm dead and laughing. You want me and I don't care. I am beyond caring about you and your fake world. Now that I'm dead I see it all clearly. I see all the bullshit. I feel better now that I don't have to get into it with you anymore. Dead man sex machine, all the ladies want me and I'm rotting in your face. You go outside and do your shit dance of fear and when you come back feeling like you have the world by the tail, look into my eyes and I'll fill you with Death. I'm dead and still dead. I'm not going anywhere. I don't change. I don't fit. I don't work and it terrifies you. I undo everything you stand for, everything you live for. You can't fuck with a dead man.

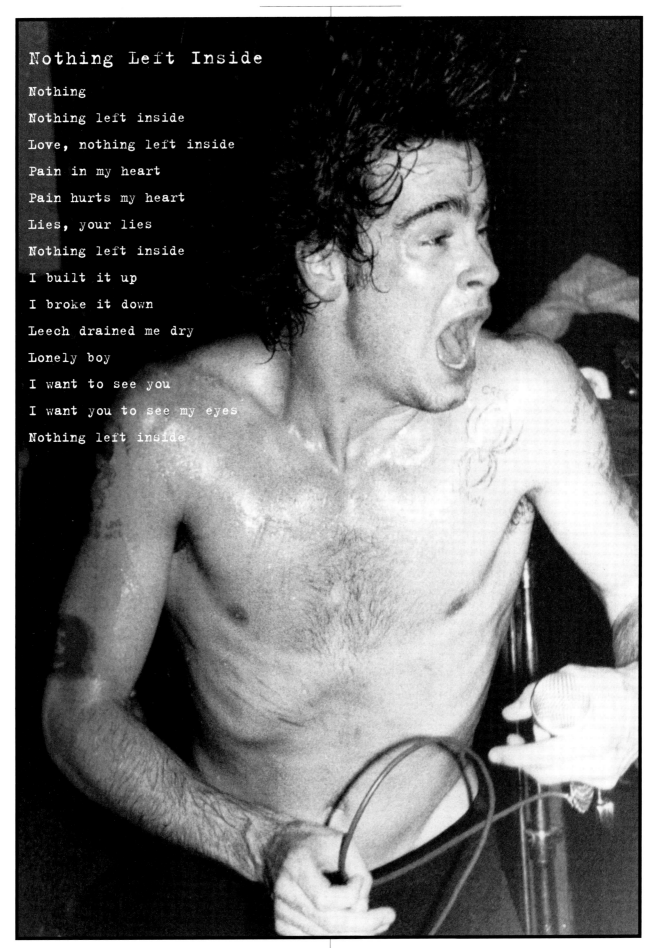

Nothing Left Inside

Nothing
Nothing left inside
Love, nothing left inside
Pain in my heart
Pain hurts my heart
Lies, your lies
Nothing left inside
I built it up
I broke it down
Leech drained me dry
Lonely boy
I want to see you
I want you to see my eyes
Nothing left inside

1983

HENRY ROLLINS

Los Angeles, 1983

Three Nights

Tonight I sit right here in my room

Going over it and over it in my mind

Something's got a hold of me

I can't shake myself loose

Let me go

I'm surely breaking up

Tonight I'm going to make that body pay

Tonight I'm going to make that body
scream

Tonight I'm going to drop to my
knees

I want to make you feel like you
make me feel

There's a lover in my heart

Killer in my hands

Someone handed me a ladder

And for the longest time

I've been climbing

To the bottom

Someone reached down and gave me
their hand

And for the longest time

I've been trying to dislodge my
teeth

I'm like a piece of shit that got
stuck on my shoe

I've been dragging that stink in the
dirt

For a long time now

I want to make you feel

Like you make me feel

I think you stuck my friend with
knives

Dragged him out so he could die

One in his heart and three in each
side

Stick me

California, 1983

Rat's Eyes

I wear rat's shoes

I pay rat's dues

I make rat's moves

I sing rat's blues

I see the world through rat's eyes

If you looked through rat's eyes

You could talk about shit real good

You would always be looking at shit

You are vermin

I want you to touch my filth

I want you to feel my filth

I want you to look into my eyes

I want you to look through my eyes

NOTES: Recorded the vocal into a lavalier, the small clip-on mic. often used on televisions shows. We clipped it to a mic stand and I went for it. Gave the vocal a strange quality that suits the lyric. A very cool Spot generated idea.

Los Angeles, 1983

Los Angeles, 1983

The Bars

There was a girl I knew
She saw the prison inside
She cursed her keeper
And swore she'd get free

Every time I see
I've got my hands wrapped around the bars
I want out right now

She made an angel's flight
Jumped out of her apartment window
And hit the street below

Every time I see
I've got my hands wrapped around the bars
I can't shut off my mind
And now I'm waiting
My hands are wrapped around the bars

I'm burning
My soul is pushed against the bars
The lie, the death behind my eyes
My mind hates my body
My body hates my soul
I close my eyes and fight inside
my own black hole

I live my life
I do my time
I realize life's lie

WORKING NOTES: Before I had moved to LA, I had never known many people who had died. After being in Black Flag for awhile, I met people who later overdosed, committed suicide or otherwise died. I met people who had done time in prisons, jails and mental institutions. It was a shock to my system that someone could be there one day and then gone the next. I never thought I would know anyone like that and then I learned that there's really no "kind" of person who dies unexpectedly or tragically.

DC, 1984

Sinking

Sinking

Wanting

Thinking

Sinking all the while

It hurts to be alone

When it hurts to be alone

When it's cold outside

HENRY ROLLINS

DC, 1985. Custom Ian MacKaye underwear displayed

When it's cold inside

When I'm feeling it

When I'm down and out

All torn up

All torn down

I'm thinking that I'm sinking

And I'm sinking all the while

Baltimore MD, 1984

Falling Down

I stand up

To fall back down

Caving in

I think my heart is caving in

Dead air

Dead phone

Dead quiet

Sinking all the while

Cutting my teeth

on the blues

Soul sinking to the

bottom of my shoes

Thinking that my life's a

waiting game

Staring at my grave and

feeling the same

When I want what I want

When I need it I need it

When all I need is all I need

I need it

Sinking

This is Good

I smash my fists into my face

I feel it

This is good

I punch the wall with my fists

I feel it

This is good

I hate to want

You make me want

I hate to want

You make me want you

I hate to want

You make me want to hurt you

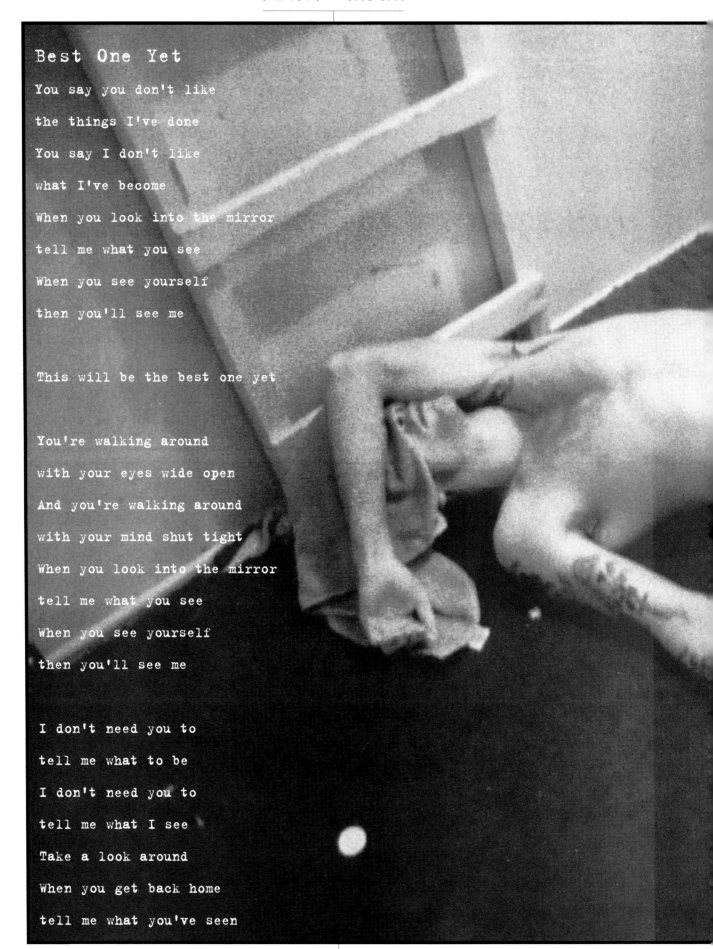

Best One Yet

You say you don't like

the things I've done

You say I don't like

what I've become

When you look into the mirror

tell me what you see

When you see yourself

then you'll see me

This will be the best one yet

You're walking around

with your eyes wide open

And you're walking around

with your mind shut tight

When you look into the mirror

tell me what you see

When you see yourself

then you'll see me

I don't need you to

tell me what to be

I don't need you to

tell me what I see

Take a look around

When you get back home

tell me what you've seen

I'm The One

I was looking for a lover

Living underneath the sun

I thought I was the other

When I knew I was the one

Caught a handle on the rising sun

Took a day to rise and fall

At the end of the journey

I was scarred and burned

But felt no pain at all

Walking through a world of lies

With a heart made out of stone

I looked deep into my eyes

And I knew I was alone

I'm a son of a son

I'm the son of the sun

My death trip

Has just begun

Paralyzed

Spinning down the drain again

Walls closing in again

Curling up inside again

No way in out up down

or otherwise again

I can't move

I can't speak

I can't shake these troubles

off of me

Trapped in and wrapped up again

Breathing in the shadows

Inward turning inward again

Paralyzed and going blind again

Wound up so tight again

My soul seeps out its pores

Paralyzed and blind

Paralyzed and going blind again

UNWELCOMED SONGS

In My Head

I hear voices when no one's around
Silent voices that no one can see

I hear voices that don't
make a sound
A distant screaming that
calls out to me
It feels so nice and hopeless
When I'm rotting in your arms
In my head
I want to be that bullet
That goes ripping throug

Sometimes strangers are
good friends of mine
They always come over w
no one's around
Strangers can sometimes
look nice in the dark
They crawl in my face and won't
leave me alone

I feel so nice and hopeless when
I'm burning through your skull
In my head
I want to be that bullet that goes
ripping through your brain
In my head

I am living in the absence of light
I've been alive inside of my skull
When I was in there I wasn't alone
Someone was laughing
and pointing at me

I'm just a killer inside of my head
The brilliance of light is
kept in the dark
I'm just a killer inside of my head
The brilliance of light is
a shot in the dark

WORKING NOTES: This was a song that Greg didn't
have any words for. It was played as an instrumental in the
studio and left at that. I worked hard to get the words to
work. This was the first time a song took me days to get
together. I almost gave up a few times.

1985

Drinking and Driving

Drink

Don't think

Drive

Kill

Get drunk a lot and work

40 hours a week

Spend half your time hungover

sick and weak

Make sure to tell yourself that

this is cool

Make sure to tell yourself that

you have no choice

1985

Make sure to tell your friends that
they drive you to it
And that you can quit any time
that you want

Party down party down drink until
you can't even see
Fill your car with your buddies and
wrap it around a tree

Feeling pretty petty lying low
in a hospital bed
Busted car busted head
you had a friend but now he's dead

WORKING NOTES: How many more people have to be turned into human garbage on the highway? The man with his brains on his pants will not be home to beat his kids tonight. Poison rips the faces of the young and turns them into shit. I watch the depression and the sag. Losers all the way to the bottom of the bottle. Not heroes, heroes don't stagger and fall on their face in the toilet. Look at them in rehab trying to live one day at a time. Pathetic wastes of time. Moderation, what the fuck does a human know about moderation? You're getting sold out every time you knock one back.

PRODUCTION NOTE:
We shot part of the video for this song in a junkyard. As the crew was setting up, I walked around and checked out the inside of the wrecked cars. I found hair, scalp and blood stuck in splintered winshields and on steering wheels, shoes on the floor. I found dried pools of blood in a couple of cars and the man told me that sometimes they get the cars in when the blood is still drying. The very talented Randy Johnson directed. He later wrote the screenplay for Oliver Stone's Doors film.

BLACK FLAG PLAYED ITS LAST SHOW IN DETROIT MI IN LATE SUMMER OF 1986

CHAPTER 3: 1986

CHAPTER 3: 1986

Geoff Clout, Henry, Hot Animal Machine sessions, Leeds UK, 1986

Black Flag broke up in late summer of 1986. I was without a band and very confused at what my next move was going to be. I was in Washington DC at the time of the split. I contacted Chris Haskett who was a long time friend and the guitar player in one of my favorite DC bands, The Enzymes. Two years previously, he and I promised each other that some day, we would record together. I called him and told him what had happened and asked if he was interested in doing something. He was. At the time he was splitting his time between America and Leeds, England. He was due back in Leeds but said he would set something up out there.

Chris went to England and I went back to LA. He called me days later and told me that he had recruited a drummer out of London named Mick Green and a bass player from DC named Bernie Wandel. Bernie and I were to fly out to England and get to Leeds. Somehow we were going to magically write a bunch of songs and make an album. ✶ ✶ ✶

Chris seemed very sure that we would have no problem coming up with material. I had my doubts. Not in him or this rhythm section I had never met, but in myself. I didn't know if I could do anything after Black Flag. It was all I had known for five years and it would be one hard act to follow and even attempting anything musical seemed like an incline too steep. There was no choice but to go so I booked a cheap flight and went to England.

I arrived in October to find the three of them at Chris' flat at 52 Harold Mount in Leeds, UK ready to go. We rented practice time at a local place and started work. There were some covers I wanted to do as we never really covered songs in Black Flag. The first song we played together was Suicide's Ghost Rider. It was really fun and after an hour, I knew we were going to at least be able to put a few songs together. We went to the practice place in the day and worked. By night, Chris and I would sit in his room and write songs. With the help of strong tea, the fearlessness that being broke and desperate instills in one combined with a strong fear of failure, we were able to string together some pretty cool songs.

Chris lived in a flat with a coin operated heater. I would go down to the freezing basement and put a pound coin in and go back to his room. We would only heat one room to make the coin last longer. Chris had this tape recording of crickets he had made the previous summer in DC. He would play it on the really damp, cold nights and the room actually seemed to warm up a little.

The days passed and we came up with more than an album's worth of material. We were going to record the songs at a very cheap studio with the idea of making a demo. After hearing how well it was going, we canceled and rebooked ourselves into a 24 track studio called Off Beat.

We dragged our gear into the room and met our engineer, a man named Geoff Clout. I remember the first day, he didn't talk to us much. I think he thought we were nuts. He seemed like a good enough guy and we figured he would warm up to us as the session went on.

We got right to work. We had little time and the budget was the small amount of money I had brought with me. Sometimes when working quickly, you turn out some great stuff. I had no label to give this to when it was done, if it was ever going to get done. We were just going for it. There was no producer so Chris and I became the "producers." I remember looking at him one day and asking, "We can do this, right?" "Of course." I suspect he didn't think so either.

We were putting down three songs a day minimum. The hours were long. It was a long way back to Chris' place and we would walk it in the dark. It was a great time.

So, a few sleep-free days later, we had 17 songs mixed. I couldn't afford to buy the master 2" tape so the multitrack no longer exists. The record cost a couple of thousand dollars to make. Geoff turned out to be one of the cooler people in existence but he still thought Chris and I were strange. Below are some of the lyrics that comprised the two records that resulted from these sessions: Hot Animal Machine and the Drive By Shooting EP.

Black And White

I've been around

Turned around

Made to see

New eyes burning in my head

Color bends

Liar friends

New eyes seeing the black and white

Ripped away

Burned away

Strength and beauty live in the

black and white

Black and white can't hide bright

light

Shining through the darkest night

New eyes hate lies

Sun blind

Everything to see

Sun light, blind light

Burned hollow, burned clean

Everything to see

Find light in dark

Blind eyes see

All the colors lie

I'm an only man

The lies hurt my mind so I think you

understand

Color driven madness was all I used

to see

Living in the black and white

Breathing in the black and white

Being what there is to be

Seeing what there is to see

Is the only thing left for me

I'm living free in the black and

white

Colors lie, try to hide

You can't hide in the black and

white

WORKING NOTES: Finally. Take the make up off and show me your real face. Take away the colored lights and the smoke and let's see you sweat. I blow your smoke away and laugh like a redneck hyena. I see you without color. I see through the smile and the covering. It's all in black and white to me. The black and white never lies, tells me what's real. The truth is all I need to know.

PRODUCTION NOTE: This was the last vocal to be done during the recording. Chris and I had mixed it as an instrumental. I could not come up with anything for the vocal. I was ready to let it go and be done with the whole thing. Chris pulled something out of one of my books and wrote a few lines down and said that I should try a vocal with this pattern. I wrote the song quickly and nailed it in a couple of takes. A good save by Chris. This song ended up being one the better songs in the 1987 set.

Lost And Found

I try to tell myself

That all this shit is going to

make me strong

But the feeling that I get

Makes me think I've been pulled along

Conviction eyes say I'm right

But the truth says to me that

I'm wrong

I try to lose myself

I'm walking down the street with my

eyes to the ground

Someone calls my name

And my head jerks back because I know

I've been found

I've got nothing to say

And they tell me to relax

They say, You're so tightly wound

I try to find myself

But I end up feeling like

someone else

I'm looking up and down

I'm lost again found again

Lost again found

I'm feeling so alone

But it seems I'm never on my own

WORKING NOTES: Can't identify with this place, any place. Every street, every face. Cold. Rather be alone. They look at me and try to read what's on my mind. They don't know me. I don't want them to know me. I'm all I've got. I won't give that away to those who would sooner throw me into the street than breathe. Lost in my room. Touch the window as the sun sets. Cold again. Walk outside and feel winter's chill. Not so bad. Less said the better. Walking to work. Limping back to the dark room. I'm trying to do the best I can but I don't know what I'm trying to do or if I'm doing ok. Silence finds me. Loneliness drains me. I don't know what keeps me here. Probably something I saw in a movie.

Followed Around

I'm being followed around again

I'm finding myself in all

the dark places

Can't see their eyes

Can't make out their faces

Feeling like an only man

Choking on a telephone line

Trying so hard but I still can't

find my mind

I'm being followed around again

Self-doubt puts a hand

on my shoulder

He says, Son you know it

only gets colder

And all the while you're

standing here

You're getting older

If you want to see the end

in my eyes

Come with me because it's right

around the corner

I'm being followed around again

NOTES: I get a phone call. Black Flag is officially broken up. Five years of my life explode. My life stares at me. I stare at the phone like it's an animal that just bit me. I take a shower and try to figure out what I am going to do with the rest of my life. I thought it was going to be Black Flag, I really did. I see that it's either sink or swim. I don't know if I have what it takes to carry on. I don't know what to do. I get out of the shower and write Followed Around. Self Doubt and Depression breathe on my neck. They rub their hands together anticipating the feast.

Hot Animal Machine I

Looking at the bottom

What do I see

I see the bottom staring back at me

You have to be Part Animal

Part Machine

If you take a look around, you can see what I mean

I won't take, I won't break

Sitting locked in a hot night prison

Going insane

I count to ten take a deep breath

Try to maintain

Bars on the window

Locks on the door

Drugs in the cabinet

Guns in the drawer

You have to be Part Animal, Part Machine

If you take a good look around

You can see what I mean

NOTES: Wrote this about living in Venice CA. I lived across the street from a crack house and there were dealers and customers outside at all hours.

No One

You were my everything

Now you're my hole in the ground

You froze me hot

Bent over all night man

Brother man

Lover man

Rubber man

Who are you looking at

Who are you trying to kill

You can't ride with us

I love you No One

I don't love you No One

Hot time's coming

Like a plague

Like a disease

When it gets hot I will get hot

I love you No One

I hate you No One

NOTES: Always there for me you never lie. You are all lover's embrace. You are all of their eyes. I always find you when I'm with her. You live inside her brain, she might not even know it. You are the eventuality I see in all of them. You are the shattering human experience. No One in my room with me. I thought I was alone. No One, the lord of suicide. Relentless witness to all human frailties. Turn it all into a ghetto. I know you can do it.

Hot Animal Machine II

I ran outside into the colored
lights
Saw all the freaks dancing in suits
Couldn't find the right words
Couldn't find the wrong words
I just wanted to kick
They looked at me
Like they never seen
Anything like that in their lives
I wanted to shove it down their
throats
I went back to my cell and freaked
out by myself
Me
Using up all of my alone
And don't you know
It feels good to know
That without a doubt
I am what I am all about
Back in my jungle
Back in my cell
Ready like a convict man
To spring into the alien combat
light
I am a man fired out of the barrel
of a gun
Instructions: Remain calm, prepare
to destroy
In my dreams they all die

Annihilation
Extermination
Incineration
In my dreams they all die
I am exterminating from the inside
No one hears the screams
No one holds the keys to my dreams
but me
The assassin of my dreams destroys
me from the inside
Without mercy, without judgment
I am the assassin of my dreams
I am the exterminator of my thoughts
I am the rust that corrodes my will
I am my worst enemy
I am my best friend, I am my end
Part Animal, Part Machine
Remain calm, prepare to destroy

UNUSED PART: Put a bullet through your bad dreams. Make the sun shine through your bad mind. I know how you feel, I've had the dreams come to kill me in my sleep too. I am my worst enemy. I don't know why I want to hurt me so much. The dreams are getting to me. They come and torment me like they own my mind. Only the stupid enjoy life to the fullest extent. Those that see through have it real bad. They're the ones who put the bullet through.

Drive By Shooting

We're gonna get in our car we're
gonna go go go
Gonna drive to a neighborhood, kill
someone we don't know
Drive by shooting
We're gonna go out killing, that's
what we're gonna do
It might be your sister or
it might be you
Drive by shooting
Sippin' on the Night Train
First gear!
Cruising down the interstate
Second gear!
Smokin' on the angel dust
Third gear!
I think my head's about to bust
Fourth gear!
Drive by shooting!
Watch out for that pig!
This is the way we get our thrills
We get in our car and
kill, kill, kill!

Drive by shooting
Got myself a heavy date!
First gear!
Don't you know I can't be late
Second gear!
Got myself a Smith and Wesson
Third gear!
Gonna teach some folks a lesson!
Fourth gear!
Drive by shooting!
Watch out for that pig!

NOTES: I thought it was about time someone wrote a pop
song about drive by shootings. As far as I knew, no one had
done it. We took it upon ourselves to write this surf-tinged
number to get the kids hoppin'.

Geoff Clout, Henry, Hot Animal Machine sessions, Leeds, UK, 1986

CHAPTER 4: 1987

CHAPTER 4: 1987

Sim, Chris, Henry, Andrew. April 1987, Trenton, NJ

Back in Venice, CA after recording in Leeds, I played the music for some people to get a reaction. I liked it but didn't know if it was any good. I played it for my friend Joe Cole and he said that it was good and that I had to tour. I never thought I would play a live show with a band ever again. I don't know why but I did. Joe said that I had to get a band together and get back out there. It was good to hear someone be encouraging and it got me pumped up. I called Chris to see if he was interested in getting a band together and getting on the road. He said he was. I told him I had an idea of who to call for bass and drums.

A few months later while in the middle of a bunch of talking shows in America, I found myself in Trenton NJ, home of Andrew and Sim, the bass player and drummer who had played with Greg Ginn in his band Gone, who opened on the 1986 tour. ✴✴✴

They were an awesome rhythm section, absolutely ultimate. I asked them what was happening with Gone and they said that Gone was no more. I gave them a tape and asked them if they wanted to be in a band with me and this guy they never met named Chris. They said sure. I was blown away. With those guys in the band, there was no way it wasn't going to work.

do some songs from the stuff that Chris and I had done, some covers and stuff that hopefully we would be able to write together.

I remember that after the first afternoon, we were playing many of the songs from the Leeds sessions very well. Within a couple of days we had some songs of our own, I think

Many phone calls and plans followed and on April 7, 1987 we had our first band practice in Sim's mother's basement in Trenton. We figured we would

Lonely might have been the first one we put together. Within a couple of weeks it was pretty strong. It had to be. We were booked to start a tour in early May with our first show April 26

First ever Rollins band show, Trenton, NJ

opening for the Circle Jerks at the City Gardens in Trenton. The pressure was on, somewhat. We practiced and wrote with a vengeance.

We did the show with the Jerks and it went down well. I remember a couple of songs in, knowing that

same studio where Chris and I worked before. Geoff was there and ready. I didn't want to produce the songs we had and I didn't want it to be a democracy in the studio. I figured that would be impossible due to everyone's

it was going to be fine. It was good to be back.

We toured through America drawing very small crowds, from 12 to 200 people a night. It was back to that. I knew that hustle well. Promoters call you into the office and explain why they won't be paying you very much more than what it will cost to get to the next town. I had been there before, wasn't all that happy to be back but there's nothing like a little bit of struggle—or a lot, to put a tiger in your tank.

By August, we were in Europe on a ten week tour. We used the opening band's soundman, a guy named Theo. He was a great soundman and a great guy and by the following year he was a member of the band.

By the end of October, the tour was over and we were in England. We had booked time in Leeds at the

strong and qualified opinions of how it should go. I called Ian MacKaye back in DC and asked if

he would produce. His talent and no bullshit approach was what the music needed and all that the budget, which was next to nothing, could bear. He just said yes and was on his way. We were damn lucky to have him on board.

We recorded very quickly. A few takes per song with very few overdubs. Thanks to great musicianship

and Ian, all songs were recorded and mixed inside of a week. The resulting songs became an album and an EP: Life Time and Do It. Cost a few grand for the whole thing to be done.

We had come a long way since April. We were a real band and we had some good songs. There was life after Black Flag after all.

Chris took some photos of us in the studio and in his room. Some of them are here.

UNWELCOMED SONGS

Lifetime sessions, Leeds UK

Geoff, Henry, Ian, Leeds UK

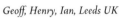

Geoff, Ian

Ian, Henry, Geoff

Ian, Henry, Leeds UK

Behold!

Sim, Leeds UK

Chris gets poked by Andrew

Ian on the mix, Leeds UK

Mixing board, Lifetime sessions

What Am I Doing Here

Walking alone on Sunset Blvd.

Feeling lonely, feeling mean,

feeling hard

Passing cars move, exhaust fumes

scar my mind

Hot night street light pressing dirt

into my eyes

Climb the stairs back

to my hollow room

Locked up, thrown away,

fallen down, sullen tomb

Voices outside screaming

Not saying a word to me

Voices inside screaming:

Hey man don't you hate hearing from me?

Turn around quick to see if I can

see my eyes

I see the face in the mirror staring

back unrecognized

Looking at my hands holding nothing,

hanging on

Feeling non existent, stuck here

feeling gone

What am I doing here?

WORKING NOTES: Walking down the blown out blvd. Looking at the dirt. Listening to the screaming car madness, wondering what the hell I'm doing here. Waiting for an answer that never comes. Go back to my room and look at the walls. I wish I could drill myself into the floor and disappear. Looking into her eyes and finding nothing. Is there any place for me at all? I think my body is a hollow

Henry, Jeffery Lee Pierce, November, London

room. Locked in-locked out, wondering what the hell I'm doing here. I can't find a reason. There must be some mis-take, wrong planet, something. They all look like strangers to me. It hurts to feel nothing. Nothing is nothing at all.

Joe Strummer, Henry, November, London

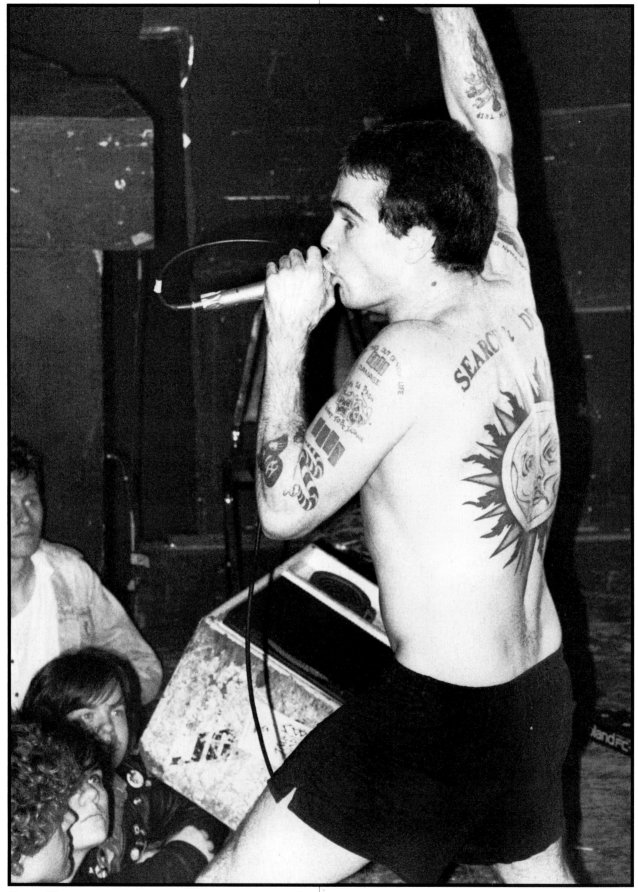

Trenton, NJ

HENRY ROLLINS

Andrew, Trenton, NJ

Chris, Trenton, NJ

Sim, Trenton, NJ

Munich, Germany

Burned Beyond Recognition

I like you, but I don't like you
I want you, but I don't want you
I need you, but I don't need you

I am one time / I am right here
I am what's left / I am right now

I touch you, but I don't touch you
I feel you, but I don't feel you
I know you, but I don't know you

I like you, but you don't like me
I want you, but you don't want me

I need you, but you
don't need me

You touch me, but you don't touch me
You feel me, but you don't feel me
You know me, but you don't know me

I remain burned beyond recognition

WORKING NOTES: What's behind your eyes? What do you really want when you say that? I know you, I know all of you, every move, every lie, every act. I don't know you, you always surprise me. All the time, new scars, new cancers in my dreams. Sometimes it's too much. Maybe the planet has too many people. Maybe they all shouldn't talk at the same time. Maybe they should take turns leaving their rooms so they wouldn't have to see so much flesh and hear so much pain. The human condition is a long scream of pain and confusion. We touch but never get close enough. The right words have not yet been invented. Love is a tired and worn out solution to human sickness. We know nothing. We are wounded. We are dying faster then we should be.

Lonely

I hate the world that

I think hates me

Punch holes in the wall

you know that hurts me

Feel dark and cold and alone

it burns me

Wish someone would come and touch me

Walking alone in the prison yard

Seeing eyes that seem to

see me so hard

Crawling like a snake

right back into my room

Feeling like a dead man

rolling around in my tomb

There's nothing like finding someone

when you're lonely

To make you want to be so all alone

Walk into a crowded room,

I start to freeze

Words fall short mouth turns to wood

It's time to leave

Never happy, never sad, iron face

Can't stop looking

I keep walking place to place

Hearing those sounds

that seem to keep me sane

Knifing eyes that point

me at my brain

Reaching out my mind it's useless

Reaching out my soul it's senseless

I feel the mute frustration when I

see your eyes

I'm inches away but in isolation it

hurts to try

I reach out my hand it turns to stone

I get up walk out the door I'm better

off alone

WORKING NOTES: It's never right. Never all the way right. You always have to shut your eyes and lie and tell yourself that you're not alone. The embrace is only temporary relief. The crowded room of strangers simultaneously attracts and alienates. You get angry with yourself at the power your confusion and blinding need pulls you towards heartbreak and letdown again and again. Sometimes you would rather window shop for friends. Keep them behind glass. Better yet, just invent them in your head and keep yourself to yourself until the next time.

America

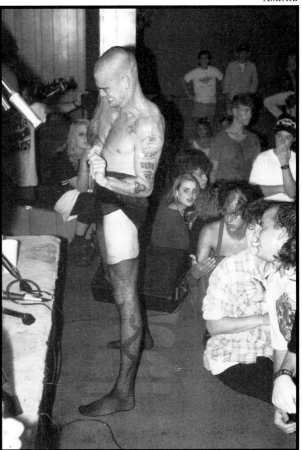

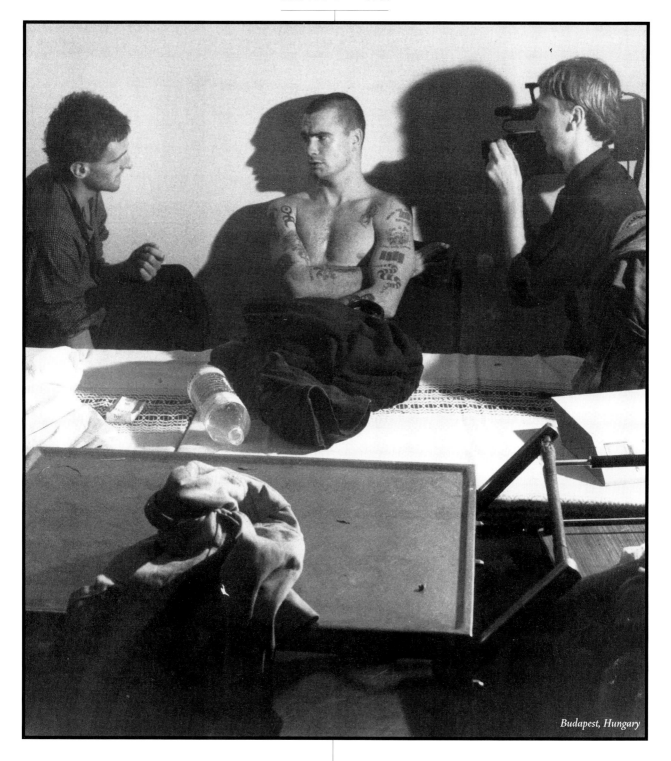

Budapest, Hungary

The Wreck Age

I take a look around me and it
makes me mad
Another friend of mine in rehab
Trying to pull himself out of
a plastic bag

He calls me from a halfway house,
says he's doing fine
Says he got himself out just in time
Says his friends would have let him
turn blue and die

Someday becomes yesterday

Chris & Henry, with members of Laibach

Your life goes and crawls away
You got a ticket on the
black train, Jack
You can't even feel the fire
on your back

Her boyfriend left her

broken and alone
She took some pills tried to crawl
to the dead zone
Her mother found her just in time
She's strapped to a bed in
psyche ward doing fine
Girl, what's happened to you,

what's going on?

Someday becomes yesterday
Your life goes and crawls away
You're walking hand in hand
with a death trip
You can't even feel the power
in its grip

Sometimes I want to take you
by your shoulders and shake
you
You've got to open your eyes, man
How long will it take you?
Walking through life blind man,
what a waste
Shut down and neutralized man,
what a case

I don't want to get stuck in
the wreck age
I don't want to go blind in

Band members with a white guy

the wreck age
I don't want to die young in
the wreck age
Sometimes it's all I can see
The wreck age is all around me
The human wreckage
To you I say goodbye

WORKING NOTES: What happens to these people?
Makes me feel like a damn fool. I wish I could have some-
how seen it coming. The helpless lies. Humans made vic-
tims of themselves. I was on the road with this one guy,
knew him for years. Last time I heard about him was some-
one telling me that he overdosed and died the day before.
That's all he gets, that's as far as it goes. All the letters I get
from people trying to get out, entire lives spent trying to
get over that first taste. One day at a time. What a begging
way to limp through life. To have to serve life instead of
taking it by its throat and living it, one is reduced to living
off it like a parasite. Hard to take when a girl comes up to
me and says hello and because of the damage of the drugs,
I cannot recognize her. The face gets hard and mummified,
the eyes sharp and distrustful. Walking dead. I'm relieved
when a guy from the old neighborhood tells me he's clean.
I don't know if I can believe him, all I can do is hope. What
a bad position to be in--to have to hope.

Turned Out

Your eyes that want to cry for me
Don't make me want to die for you
Your arms that want to wrap around me
Don't make me want to hang around you
Your bleeding heart that wants to
bleed me
Can't make me think I want or need you
And it's no wonder anymore
That I don't wonder anymore

I've been turned out

You tell me you're my friend
You say I know you
I'll trust you just as far as
I can throw you
Now I don't know you,
I know my enemies
You know they look at me
with honest eyes
They hate my guts but at least
it's the truth
I'll trust them
just as far as I
can throw them off
a roof

I'm no stranger to kindness
I've never missed the fist that
kissed my face
I'm no stranger to cheapness
I never came to love the push
and shove
Steel glass eyed cities
Flash dirty smiles when they see me
Open their filthy arms to greet me
I don't know if they want to kiss
or kill me

WORKING NOTES: Whatever you're going to do, just shut the fuck up and do it. Play your fucking music, smell the shitty air, deal with the clubs. What the fuck are you going to do to me besides kill me? That's the bottom line. That's all there is left. Love me, hate me, don't fool yourself and think that it matters. It doesn't. After you're gone, no one will care. When I'm gone, no one will notice. I don't want to be your friend. It's all in your mind. I will never be there for you. I have been strip-mined by cities and the nights. They always get the best of me because they're the only thing that I ever respected. Your embrace has always been too shallow.

Munich, Germany

1000 Times Blind

1000 times blind
See me falling see me hit the floor
1000 times blind
See me falling see me lose my mind

Don't touch me – you'll cut yourself
Don't find me – you'll lose yourself
Don't love me – you'll hate yourself
Don't hold me – you'll drop yourself

1000 times blind
See me throw myself to the floor
1000 faces looking back at you
1000 times blind

I reach inside – I can't feel myself
I open my eyes – I can't see myself

I scream out loud –
I can't hear myself
I try to recognize –
I don't know myself

1000 times blind
I get cut off from myself
Smashed up, cut up
1000 pieces
1000 times blind

WORKING NOTES: 1000 times blind. Glass breaks glass, watch me shatter. See me lying on the floor scattered in pieces. Don't look too closely, you might see yourself. Glass cuts glass, see me lying in 1000 pieces. 1000 eyes staring back at you. You see yourself 1000 times and you get cut up on yourself. Glass makes glass bleed. You get cut off from yourself. So many ways to lie and not know. So many ways to hurt someone and not know how much damage you cause. Perception cripples and ruins. What you see comes back to rip your guts out. Looking out at them, their eyes reflected in light. Wondering what they see. Never getting close enough. The "I" in the eye. What is sight? Do I really see them? Can I see myself? Would I recognize myself in passing? Do I know when I'm lying? Do I know another's truth? 1000 times blind.

You Look At You

Killing myself again
Losing to myself again
Living in a dream again
Living on a lie again

I've got to do something and I've got to do it now
I've got to get to something but I know I don't know how
Always keeping busy taking other people's chances
I know I know the question but I'm too afraid to ask it

Lying to myself again
Forgetting my name again
Hating my guts again
Burning my friends again

You look at you

Losing my grip again
Starting to slip again
Standing in line again
Losing my mind again

Always looking for myself in
all the people that I see
Wonder what they're seeing when
they're looking back at me
I'll tell you that I hate you but
you know that's just a lie
You know that I don't mean it
I'm the one that I despise
Can you deal with it?
Deal with it

WORKING NOTES: I can't deal with it so I'll give it to you. Get off my back. It's my life on your time. I screw it up for myself and I'm glad you're around so I'll have someone to blame. I need you because I can't get the strength to see myself. I'll never fail. I'll always find something about you that's fucked. Somehow I always manage to escape the jaws. Wait a minute, stop the clock. You look at you.

People Like Me

People like me have no friends
People like me are human alienators
People like me come and go alone
People like me die forgotten
in darkness
People like me don't wait for
the phone to ring
People like me, what a joke —
there are no people like me

People like me don't reach out
People like me don't want to know you
People like me are obsessed
with their pain
People like me can't feel
People like me can't see
People like me, what a lie —
there are no people like me

People like me don't hold back
People like me don't hold on
People like me are too empty to hate
People like me feel like dying
at all times
People like me are the impossibility
People like me, what a drag —
there are no people like me

WORKING NOTES: You can get lost on Earth. Watch them crawl. They have nothing to do with you. Sometimes the dark room is the only answer. If I said it out loud they would laugh and tell me to cut the shit, that's why I keep the strangeness to myself. I walked the streets of Copenhagen, looked into the gray river from a bridge. I knew I was right. I watched them pass by. I pulled the cold air into my lungs. Soon it would be tobacco smoke and a bunch of strangers telling me to hurry up. I know I have to be strong in my strangeness. Can't take any of them on for the ride. There are no people like me. Earth is huge. A ruined, sprawl with a knife in its back. Everyone is a damn fool.

CHAPTER 5: 1988-1989

CHAPTER 5: 1988-1989

Belgium, 1988

This was a rough patch. We were playing ok and getting along fairly well but it was hard to stay fed and keep the rent paid. The day-to-day started to grind on us all. But even then, the music was strong and there were gigs for us so we played. Little money, no money, negative money, we kept playing and somehow we all paid the rent on our small rooms that went month after month unoccupied as we stayed out.

We played hard every night and the music sustained us. 1988 was the year I understood without a doubt there was always going to be tension in this band. I had been there before. ✳✳✳

Hard Volume Album

It was late 1988. We had a tour starting in early 1989 in Australia and wanted to try and record our next album before we left the country.

Our manager/lawyer Gail suggested we check out a studio her friend Rae worked at called Echo Sound. They might be able to cut a deal as they had nothing happening at the time and were looking for work. Chris and I went over there and Rae gave us the tour of the place. It was small and not all that geared for rock music. It was more about the rap thing, I think Eazy E had just been in there. The rooms were small but Rae could cut us a great deal and there were many nights we could use both rooms at once. We agreed to work there.

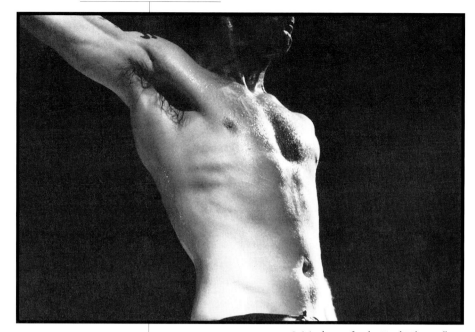

Original cover for the Hard Volume album

Andrew and Sim came out with the gear from NJ. The band went into a brief rehearsal period before heading into the studio. We wrote Tearing, You Didn't Need and What Do You Do during this time.

Living accommodations for the lads was the floor at my place, my roommate nor my bandmates were all too happy about this but everyone put up with it. I was living in a bad house in Silverlake near downtown. The house had paper-thin walls and no room for two people much less Andrew, Sim and Theo included. Chris luckily had an equally dismal living space a few blocks away but at least it wasn't as heavily populated as mine.

Once in the studio, the band was not happy with the cramped quarters and the fact that the drums had to be set up so far from the rest of the band. We had made a mistake coming to this place but there we were. Everyone was grumbling but pitched in and worked hard nonetheless.

At one point, we couldn't use the other room because there was a rap session going on in there. I don't know who it was. These guys saw fit to use our studio as their lounge. One night, all these intense gangster types just came in and sat down. None of them said a word to us. They just opened up bottles of malt liquor, fired up joints and glared at us. As soon as they heard a little of our music, they all cleared out. I think we harshed their mellow.

Budapest, Hungary 1989

We worked on the album relentlessly all the way up to the day we left for Australia. Theo was still mixing I Feel Like This until about three hours before the flight.

When I handed in the final sequence for the album to the record company, they asked why Tearing and You Didn't Need were not included. I told them that they were not ready yet. In truth they were not all they could be at that point but the main reason I left those off the record was because I knew that I was going to be on a differ-

Phil "The Crusher" Thain, Henry

Berlin, Germany

I developed strep throat from overwork and general exhaustion. While we were working in the studio, I was getting all the paperwork and freighting agreements together for our upcoming Australian tour. Between that, the studio and the general stress of the band at that time, my body folded on me. It made doing vocals difficult. On the recordings, you can hear that my voice is maxed out.

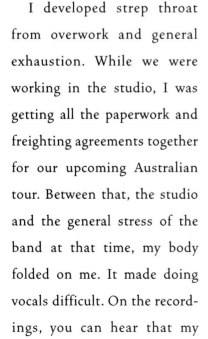

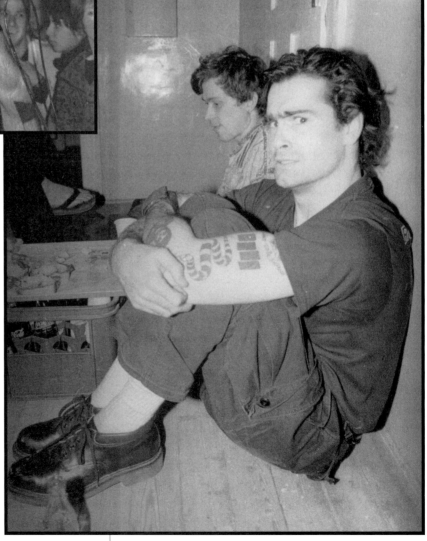

ent label next time around so why waste good songs on a record that was going to get poorly attended to? They would get their chance the next time around. It was one of the first times that I practiced anything resembling restraint in a business situation.

Re-recorded versions of those songs showed up on The End of Silence. The Hard Volume versions were eventually released on the re-mastered edition of Hard Volume.

This was to be the way of future Rollins Band recording sessions. Tension, dissension, grumbling. The pain in the ass of making the Hard Volume record was nothing compared with what was to come. One last note on this topic. The title Hard Volume comes from a radio playlist I saw in Europe that year where we were placed in that

particular category. I figured that it was a good name for a record. Two cool words, easy to remember.

Hard

It's hard to get by
It's hard to get through
It's hard to hear me
when I'm talking to you
You see these hard eyes
you know what I mean
These eyes got hard
after what they've seen
I am that hard man so good to find
I am that hard man
with the iron mind

I got hard and I stayed hard
You can't keep me down
because I'm hard
I keep moving because I'm hard
I keep burning because I'm hard
I'm going over not getting by
Hard sense makes sense

Real pain is what I reach
The real thing is what I keep
I am because I am hard
I will because I am hard

WORKING NOTES: To understand change. To move forward when it seems impossible. To be able to maintain under stress. To be kind when conditions are strained. To be destructive and indestructible. There's reasons that some things seem too easy, beware. On your way to work, school. Having to look at them, to deal with them, one must be hard. Every morning 0600, uniform on, out the door by 0630. Long bus ride to school. Forced to listen to these future overweight slobs tell me that I'm going to be their driver. Telling me that I'm a freak. Inhale their abuse. Exhale car exhaust into their faces as I leave them in their pathetic rut. They can't make me want it. A sun that continues to rise in height and temperature for a life time until it finally explodes.

Down and Away

I close my eyes and I look inside
I realize I'm a bad place
I am the last place that I want to be
I open my eyes and I want to get away
Push me pull me ripping myself apart
I want to run, I want to hide
But I can't get away

I can't get in
I can't get out
I can't get to myself
So I can get to you
I can't get close
When I'm close to you
I can't get through myself
So I can get to you
The closer you get
The farther away I feel
The closer I get
The farther away you feel

If you could touch me and
I could feel it
I'd want you to touch me so
I could feel it

I'm dead as I fall through your eyes
I am the prisoner trapped in life
I am the loser in the game I play
I am the garbage that I throw away
I'm not at home in the place I stay
I can't understand why
I got thrown in a hole
Down and away

WORKING NOTES: Don't touch me. I'll only let you down. I'll freeze your blood like life freezes mine. I ran my hands over her naked body. I felt nothing. I wasn't alive in her world. She asked me what the matter was. I had no answer. She said I was a bastard. I never saw her again. I can't get too close. I get close and then it gets dark and I am a different animal than you. I can't identify. Your touch means nothing to me. I am not of your world. Mine accepts no one. The closer you get the farther away I feel.

No

Break it

I don't need your lovely

I don't want your beauty

I pull back in my head

I load ugly in my head

This world is bloated — it's ugly

A sprawling ghetto — it's ugly

See him walking with a gun in his hand

See her walking with a gun in her hand

See me walking with a gun in my heart

Loaded ugly

Planet Joe

I don't need no friend to tell me

who my friends are

I don't need some pig to tell me

what the rules are

See me walking — I'm loaded

I've got an ear for every sound

I've got an ear down to the ground

The blues come down stone by stone

The streets are burning

The years are turning

The sky is falling down

The line is being drawn

Been pushed too far

Been pushed too hard

Locked down

Knocked down

WORKING NOTES: It's ugly. I'm ugly. The real thing is ugly. Up close. Touch me. I'm real. Look at me. I'm ugly. When you get close it's ugly. Into the flesh ugly. Live it. It's you, it's me, it's ugly. These people, tiny masters, hollow men. See them rush forward trying to blow your mind with numbers, with blood displays and statistics. See them try to pull you into their useless world. They try to overwhelm you with bright lights and loud noises. It's a wall of sound that picks your pockets when you're not looking. They'll always give you something good to look at while they work you over. They seek to intimidate you into a lifelong career of submission. If they can, they will reduce you to an example of fearful human garbage. They will pull you into the shit river and drown you. Not this time. Fuck you.

1-16-89 SYDNEY AUS.

break myself in two
I feel like I want to
feel just like you
Can you feel it like I feel it
Do you feel it like I feel it
I feel like this

WORKING NOTES: Why did he stab her thirty-five times in the front seat of his car? For the same reason that they got married. The shrink used to ask me what the problem was. Words didn't work. I should have bashed her in the face with the ashtray and maybe she would have understood how I felt. Fuck talking. Turn that fucking thing off.

I Feel Like This

I feel like this
I feel like I want to

What Have I Got

I've got a wantless need
I've got a thoughtless mind
I've got a needless want
I can't unwind

I've got a heart that hates
I've got hands that like to break
They tell me to hold on
They never let me go
I am a clenched fist
Looking for a wall to kiss
I am a locked door looking
For a foot to kick me to the floor

What have I got
I've get everything
What have I got
Nothing much at all

Self-rejected, well protected
Too locked up inside myself
to ever get free
Frustrated, self-hated my hands
turn to fists
Violence so hard to resist
I get so mad
I do things that I regret
So stupid but not stupid enough
To ever forget

Got no name got no brain
In my heart I feel no pain
I've got music pounding in my head

Stop looking start looking
You better look out
I'm not feeling too nice today
Can't be late, can't relate
Don't take my time,
don't give me your hate
I've got enough of my own
I can't stop, I can't start
It holds me together while
it tears me apart

WORKING NOTES: Straight jacket, padded cell, long line, treadmill, self-doubt. Hands full of nothing. Head full of water. Lungs full of hot air. Words full of hollow. Endless tail chase. Zero to zero. Truckload of frustration. Two days a week to the head shrink. Asking all the questions that have no answers. What's your problem? She had her office in the basement of her house. Her children used to come by and laugh in my face. What's your problem? My head is on fire. The mouth looks for words to fire like a cannon, like a gun. The music plays the body, slave to electricity. Locked in the room for years with electricity. It plays me like a bolt of lightning.

Holland

Love Song

```
I want you

I hate you

Put your hands on me

Put your mouth on me

Touch me

Make me real

I don't want you

because I hate you

I hate you because I want you
```

WORKING NOTES: I want what I can't have. If I get it I don't want it anymore. If I get it, I want to render it useless so no one else will be able to use it. I want to ruin it, run it down, destroy it. I want you. I want all of you, every pore. Soon as I get it I'll be gone.

The Idiot sought her for years. She would notice him enough to allow him to fill his mind with fantasies of how it could be. She was always just out of reach. The Idiot followed her for years. He frustrated and humiliated himself over her. He began to hate her. He thought of humiliating her. He wrote down ways to be cruel to her. He went out of his way to hurt her feelings. She never understood why he did this. He wanted her. He hated her. His life was spent as a breathing fist.

Monica, Henry

Henry, Mick Harvey, Kid Congo, Chris Haskett

Turned Inside Out

Turned inside out for all to see

Touch this

Feel this

See yourself

See the monster

Feel the beast

Laugh out loud

Say: Freak

Take this

Break this

Your passion

Pure criminal

Is that you, could that be you?

Filthy

Pathetic

Liar

Sadist

Villain

Freak

Turned inside out for all to see

See until your eyes find you

See until your eyes blind you

Beautiful killer

I wait for you to rise

Get up

Entertain me

Laughing as you fall

Flashing

I sing love songs to the abyss

It sings back to me:

Ha ha

Who's the criminal now?

Is that you?

Could that be you?

Turned inside out for all to see

WORKING NOTES: A man stands in a crowded public park on Saturday afternoon. He takes off his clothes. Everyone stares. He produces a knife and stabs himself hard in the breast bone and saws a six inch gash in himself. He drops the knife and inserts his fingers into the wound. He wraps his fingers around his ribs and pulls. The ribs and skin pull back. All of his entrails fall out onto the grass. He keeps pulling until the ribs are wrapped around his back. He stares back at them.

PRODUCTION NOTE: The track Turned Inside Out started as an instrumental jam that the guys did in the studio when we were laying down tracks for the Hard Volume album. I had only heard it once and forgotten about it. Theo called from the studio and asked if I wanted to come in and try to put a vocal on it. I said I would give it a try but had no idea what to do with it. The above image came to mind and I wrote it down. From that, I wrote down "Turned inside out, filthy, criminal, pathetic," and went in. Theo played a few minutes of the track and I looked at the paper and went for it. I sang until the tape ran out, one take improvised.

You Didn't Need

You turned me in and you burned me out

You pulled me in and you locked me out

You ripped your feelings

right across my back

You didn't see that I was bleeding

You turned away when I spoke

right to you

You looked away when I

looked right through you

You didn't need to do that to me

When I touched you

Did you feel it?

Did you ever feel anything at all?

Do you ever lie awake at night?

Do you ever think of me?

I've got my arms wrapped

around myself

You've got your arms

around someone else

I try to tell myself

I'm not down

I didn't want it but I got it anyway

I didn't want it and I couldn't

get away

I can't deny it

I miss you

Even though it hurts inside

In my dreams I kiss you

I keep a lie alive

I wrack my brain trying to remember

Anything I did to you

I wreck my brain trying to dismember

Any part attached to you

I'm sorry I still feel

this pain inside

It shows on my face like a scar

It's something I can't hide

Some people are better left alone

It hurts so much when you have

nothing to say

It hurts so much to have to walk away

WORKING NOTES: Man in love slips and falls out, falls long and hard gets up and becomes a victim of love. Blind and stupid from pain, lashes out, blames anyone, everyone. Too painful to look inside and face that face. Cries out through newly acquired bitter tasting victim's mouth. Easy to fall in, hard to get out.

I wish I could have read your mind. What made you do what you did? You left me hanging and then you left me. I still think about you. It will take me a long time to get over it. I can't understand why you acted like that. You with your wooden heart. You with your fancy words you didn't know how to use. Was I just someone you fucked? Do you ever think of me? Was I just a fill-in? Why weren't you straight with me? I would like to know the way you think. Do you know the feeling of being with someone and at the same time being all by yourself? Did it ever bother you or did it feel like all the other times? You'll never hear from me again. You think I'm going to try to talk to you and make an idiot out of myself even more than I already have? I just don't understand and it hurts. I liked you and because of it I got a hole in me. Do you know what you do to others?

Tearing

The way you look at me
Is tearing me apart
And the way I make you feel
Is tearing you apart
And the things we're doing
to each other
Is tearing us apart
Look at you and me,
tearing each other apart
I don't mean to do it
You don't mean to do it
So we better stop it now
Because we're tearing
each other apart

It's hard to be alone
But it's harder to be with you
I'm a lying liar with my
pants in fire
Tearing myself apart
Slamming down the phone
right in your face
Tearing you apart
So close, too close, not close enough
Tearing each other apart
When I see you
I want to tell you
But then I lose the words
And it tears me apart

Better walk away
Before we crawl away
I've got a hole inside

And I keep it deep inside
And I'm going to go inside
And it's there I'm going to hide
Because I've got to get away
To see if I'm ok
Sometimes things don't work out
It tears you apart, it tears me apart
Sometimes happens all the time
And I'm feeling torn apart

What Do You Do

When no one will listen and
time won't wait
When you see yourself and
see the one that you hate
When the night lasts forever
and times stands still
When you see yourself and
want to kill
When the world doesn't fit
the head on your shoulders
When you punch the walls and
feel the world's fist
The big ideas you had leave you

feeling so small
I can see it in your eyes,
you can't deal with it all

What do you do when you
want to get over
What do you do when you
want to get through
What do you do when you
just can't take it
What do you do when you
just can't fake it anymore

Feel the pressure
Feel it squeeze
The eyes in your head
The heart in your chest
Where's the answer
Where's the release
What do you do

When the lies they told and
the price that you paid
Force you to see the mistake
that you made
When they shake your hand and

stab your back
When frustration paints your
four walls black
When they pick you up and let you fall
When you find their something
is nothing at all
When ends miss ends and the
endlessness sends you
Down to the bottom of the
drain in pain
When you're pushed to the edge
and can't maintain

Hot Animal Machine III

Can't separate intent from intention

Walk among them as you would killers

Watch out for the disease

The television screams louder

The call up, the hang up

They will give you the send up

And they will put the needle in

They are filth magic don't

underestimate them

They are not your friends

Are you on a mission or are you

standing in line?

Pin pupil eyed girl shooting up

in my bathroom

Telling me she's clean

No one gets clean until they

kill all the monkeys

I am the end of hope –

I hear you crying

I am the end of hopelessness –

I see you dying

Wake up or don't

Gun in your mouth –

I hear you calling

Addicted to a new thing –

I see you crawling

Get up or don't

If you don't have eyes in the back of

your head – You better grow some

If you're holding back your strength

– You better show some

Haven't you heard the new

machine gun music?

I told you about

Part Animal Part Machine

I got my eyes wide open —

I've seen what I've seen

It's the real thing —

I'm not dreaming

If you turn your blind side outside

You get taken for a long ride

down slide

You got to dare to be aware —

Don't pretend it's not there

Lock and load don't explode

They want you to blame,

they want you insane

You've got to maintain

When I speak I'm outspoken

Straight up back unbroken

When you follow you swallow

and wallow in their game

When you go the other way,

it's their way

It's the same game with

a different name

I'm not crazy

I'm clear eyed wide awake

I'm packing a loaded idea

The safety switch is off

As You Get Screwed

You make me weary
You never stop
But you don't know what you're doing
And you don't know who you are
You're a voo doo doll
They're sticking you full of holes
You're bleeding to death and
you can't feel it
You think you're playing a game
But you're getting played anyway
Every day, every way
And you get destroyed piece by piece
You think you're really something

With your air-conditioned
Designer drug convenience sex
Your parents are color
television sets
And you've been running, lying
Cheap thrilling, slumming, scamming
Leaching, screwing, backstabbing
Talking about sacrifice
You're bought and sold daily
You don't even own your thoughts
Your dreams are rented, secondhand
You're jewel-eyed cruel-mouthed
Glittering on some fat man's hand
You're nothing

A sad vacancy

You go home to a home that

you don't own

You got your friends hanging

around your neck

Sucking you dry

You're beautiful but your eyes

are going nowhere

At the end of the day you got nothing

They dress you up

Make your face up

Make your mind up

And then they wind you up

Turn you loose in their front yard

And tell you the world is yours

I can't say that it brings me down

Passing the time while time

passes you

As you get screwed

WORKING NOTES: I never told you how stupid you were. If I had really loved you I would have told you for your own good. You should go back to the small shit town you came from before they take you all the way. Already they have you on their schedule, their value system, you wait eagerly for the guy who tried to fuck you in his office to give you one more chance, all of a sudden it doesn't seem like such a bad thing to fuck the guy. Might get your foot in the door, right? I will never forget all the words you used to use thinking you were so smart. I should have told you to get a dictionary so you could see how fucking stupid you were. I see you from time to time, you always have a new bullshit story to go along with the one about how one of your friends just died in his apartment from overdosing. How far do you think you are from the same thing? You're owned and you don't even know it. I still think of you. Somewhere inside there's a real heart that beats. I don't think you would feel it if it jumped out of your throat and fell on your plate.

Monkey

I tried to talk to you the other day
But your monkey said you had
nothing to say
I tried to touch you the other day
But your monkey slapped my hand away

I try to get close to you
But your monkey keeps the distance
I try to get him away from you
But your monkey maintains
the distance

You called me up the other day
And asked to borrow some money
I asked you if you needed help
You said you were cool but

the monkey was hungry

How can you say he loves you
When he leaves you with
all those bruises
You must need him really bad
To make up all these lies
and excuses

The choice was made
The hand was played
You should have stayed
But you went away with your monkey

Yesterday I went to your door
The monkey said you weren't
around anymore

All The Same

They come from different places

They all have different faces

But at the end of the day

They're all the same

Some are mad

Some are sad

Some are good

Some are bad

Rich poor honest liars

I know what I know

They all play a game

And they're all the same

They talk about change

But they never change

Year after year

Time after time

It's the same old rhyme

They hold me down

They drive me insane

They're all the same

They always talk to me

Telling me how it's going to be different

It always feels the same

I look into their eyes

It's the same thing

Inside I laugh

They don't impress depress or

intimidate me

They don't make me feel

anything at all

WORKING NOTES: Like they could ever breathe life. Feed the Machine. Wake it up, make it scream. Try to use a little style as you pass through the needle's eye. You play act in front of the mirror. You dance alone. You want to kill, you want to taste human flesh. You want to go to hell for the weekend. If you could you would be the boss and make them all pay and then turn it all around so you could be the hero before they all found out the truth about you. The dead walk the streets on their way to work. That's just the way it is around here.

Freak

I'm a freak, touch me
There must be something wrong
When I look at you,
I look into my eyes
When you tell me how you feel,
I understand
I've felt those things before too
But then you point your finger at me
and say: Freak
You push me away
You lie to yourself
You tell yourself that
you're different
That I am something below you,
obscene
A filthy stranger you know so well
I am a freak
You feel what I feel
Touch me
I'm a freak in the hot house
Shaking this heat, this night
The air is peeling the paint
off my soul
You hear me screaming, it's real
This numbered animal is
singing your song
This freak is doing it to death
Doing the death shuffle
Hearing black trains
Torching myself inside my brain
I'm choking the life out of life
Ripping it out of me and
giving it to you

I want to see what you're going to
do with my life
Now that it's at your feet

WORKING NOTES: I'm a freak touch me. Let me show you an animal. Touch me, help me destroy myself. Shake me, I feel dead. I need things that hurt. I am addicted to life. You have the fix burning in your eyes. Let me burn to cinder right in front of you. Look at me, this plagued body. Touch me tonight in this room. Start another war inside me. Let me lose it all. I want to crawl. This is the only song I know. Let me sing for you. Start me up. Let me incinerate for you.

Chainsnake Blues

I see the end

From the start I see the end

When I look into your eyes

I see the end looking back at me

When I look at my life

I see the end

I taste termination,

it's in my blood

I was born to terminate

The blood roars I hear it pounding

My eyes see through and see through

The scars on my flesh make me see

the end

When you touch me

When you surround me

I see the end in your

beautiful mortality

In the night's morning when I rise

I get up to take the end's ride

You can't break a dead man's heart

Through this night no dusty tears

fall from my face

Endless black light

Chainsnake night

I crawl to my place

I know who I am

I am the Chainsnake man

My back won't break

My eyes won't close

I crawl, I can't fall

I can't die no matter how hard I try

Life is ugly and so am I

You can't love me because I don't

My heart doesn't beat

It just refuses to stop

I am the Chainsnake man

WORKING NOTES: Look at the snake crawl by. Look at those scars. You want to touch him. You can't bring your hand to its skin. You are repulsed yet fascinated. Look at the flesh, burned bright by sunlight. Frozen solid by cold night. Eyes that never close. Chainsnake, spit on, shit on, lied to and stepped on. Still keeps crawling down the trail. Snake made of chain, snake made of steel. Doesn't love, hate or feel. Has no hands to greet you, no legs to run on. Always crawled, always will.

Thin Air

The night falls

Shadows join me

My room becomes a cell

The walls define me

The silence pounds me

It holds me down

Depression grabs me

And pulls me down

Solitude becomes the weapon I use

A knife that cuts me and

cuts me smooth

I got a new identity

I become my enemy

A big part of me so seldom seen

No one lies to myself like I do

To myself in my room

The silence howls in my ear

The deafening roar becomes so clear

I'm drowning in thin air

The more I think - the more I hate

I hate myself

I sit still but I turn on myself

The night is endless and so am I

When I'm lost in myself

When I lie to myself

I kill my soul piece by piece

I feel myself slipping

Common sense fails me

Existence flails me

Guilt trips nail me

I'm here starving in my room

Eating myself cell by cell

My eyes stretching wall to

wall to wall to wall

When I'm left to myself

I keep myself to myself

When I'm here by myself

I cut myself on myself

It's nothing - I'm nothing

I'm breathing in thin air

I'm choking on thin air

Losing my breath in thin air

WORKING NOTES: I watch the wall, the wall watches me. We stare into each other's eyes. It's a paranoia game I play with myself. The air gets thin as the night passes blades underneath my skin. If I could pull my brain out I'd taste a bit to see what it's like. If I could dissect the night instead of myself, I would. I always turn on myself without fail. Waiting like an idiot for someone to pull me out of the mess I got myself into by breathing. I always end up alone. I use it as an excuse to murder my mind.

NOTE: This song got as far as a demo recorded in summer 1988. We played it live a few times and then dropped it. The demo version has been released on the Hard Volume re-master.

She

She is blues music

She is the holes that I

punch in the walls

I see a black shape in my dreams

Behold

She has appeared

She is the unmoving carved out nights

She is the slow passing of time

She is tonight right now

I am burning

WORKING NOTES: Rape. Broken jaws and heartache. Blues music is born. Sadness that melts prison bars, but not enough to escape. Evil. Poison. Waste. Ghetto for the heart. I don't wonder why anymore. I thought I was above it all. I see that I'm wrong, so wrong. Packing all the scars to prove my stupidity. Serial killing sprees. Whole lotta love. Rotting in the trunk. Too much booze and broken dreams. Never gets better, gets worse with age. The most beautiful thing there is to some. Something to fear and loathe for others. Beauty is a weapon that gets used against the one who possesses it. Ladies getting their faces broken. No one will remember your name at the end of the blood bath. You were once a prized object. You will be again.

You

You

I see you everywhere

I know you are aware

You watch me as I stare

I know

It gets so hard to hide

The things I feel inside

Feelings never lie

Please stay here for awhile

I want to see you smile
I want to know your name

So hard to be alone
I thought I was made of stone
You show me that I'm wrong

I know you feel it too
You feel it because it's true
There's no need to be afraid

It's so damn cold in here
I burn to have you near
Please hurry

I scream for your embrace
How long will I have to wait
I know you need it too

Please make what's inside real
It gets so hard to feel
I need to be alive

I know you understand
You know your soul's demand
You feel your heart's command

Jungle Blues

At night I have dreams
Dreams of the jungle
Full of death
Full of fire
Nightmares, horror

Rivers of blood
Bodies ripped apart
Burned half-naked
Face down on the mud
The jungle comes alive
Moves like an animal
Changes form, stalks me
Night after night I slept
inside its belly
Shadows
Something's always moving
in the shadows
They might try to get me
If I could see them I could kill them
I can't identify
I see through them
I put on a face, I wear a mask
They don't like to look at me
They say I make them feel cold inside
I see death everywhere
I can smell it
I have touched its hand
It felt like mine
I walked along the wall and looked at
the names
I could smell the death
I could see the smoldering piles
I saw Death's face smile
I'm being followed
I'm ready to kill
Anyone of them could be the enemy
I am not afraid of Death
I can't wait
End this pain

Still Human After All These Years

You never knew they could be so cruel

Telling you to let love rule

While you're sleeping

They tighten the chains that are

keeping you down

Taking you mind

Wasting your time

Making you blind

When they smile don't be fooled

Cut through with action

Get satisfaction in the truth

That is hard

But hard is good

This is something that

must be understood

Life —

part animal part machine is real

Not a dream state

Before you pass, wipe the slate clean

Don't sell out

See the lost that fell out

Down by the wayside

Taken for a bad ride

Ate the poison and swallowed the lie

On channel 7 at 8 o'clock

you watch them die

Year after year with

a blind eye you cry

And a deaf ear you hear

Never thinking

That they want to be sinking

Their fangs into you

You tell yourself that
you're the best
When really you're just another test
The one they call when they yell,
"Next!"
Getting broken and beaten and
all of the while
They poke and provoke you and keep
you on file
Watching you
Where you go
What you do
Who you know
Protecting and serving and wracking
your brain
We have places for people like you
they explain
You're better off letting someone
else do the driving
They'll leave you just able
to survive
Shaking and scared so glad
to be alive
Heart full of rage, reaching
for the twelve gauge
Looking to make tomorrow's front page
Sowing the seeds of destruction
Spoken token and social role
Fill out the required function
As you sit in your hole
As you ride the downside
Of this critical mass
Criminal mind
Go to the head of the class

Hatred's Clown

Rage keeps me down
I am hatred's clown
I am blind inside
Choked on human pride
I go run and hide
So stupid I can't see

I think I'm always right
I lose sleep at night
My dreams haunt me
Loser when I play
Lying when I say
Nothing gets to me
Truth trips me out
Reality makes me shout
When is enough enough?
Too much too long
Too hard too strong

Lost mad mean sad hurt
Feeling like old dirt
Confused beyond belief
Low mind unkind
Refuse to find relief

Here in my solitary space
Wearing my clown face
I hold onto myself
I hold myself prisoner

Human Blues

Deficiency, doubt, dependency
Violence, trickery, letdown
Expectation, lies, help
Self destruction, desperation, abuse
Insomnia, reproductive psychosis
Alienation, self-infliction
Open the chasm
Explore the wound
Surrender to the abyss
Up to your neck in humanity
Sinking fast
Pain inside you can't contain it
Feelings find you alien
You can't explain it

Walking lost found a way to choose
Placed your bets set yourself up
to lose
Won out and shut yourself down
Personal price was your self expense
Smashed out on the bottom
Choking on shards of experience
A shattered dream walking point with
the human blues

Aspiring to a plastic vision
Unattainable value you tricked
yourself insane
Watching the window to see if
they're watching
Deep in the skin jungle
The embryos sleep with guns
in their hearts

You want to find yourself
a part of it
So you can say it wasn't a waste
Damaged goods feeling bad in the
human blues

WORKING NOTES: Life sticks in my throat. Shoves glass under my skin. Drags me through the coals of thick and thin. Life has bad breath and doesn't care. You want to see human nature unmasked and unguarded? Go study the insect world. Body found folded in a suitcase, cut in pieces. Who did this, space aliens? No, someone with a lot of the same characteristics that you have. Life injects meat with a curse. Civilization needs shock treatment. Rapists, movie stars, serial killers, everyone has their own fan club and cheering section. It's all the blues to me. Every mother and child, every pig, every human act. I've got my arm down my own throat trying to rip the beast out of my guts.

Terminal Man/
Terminal Woman

I am a terminal man
I've always got a fist in my hand
She makes me crawl
She makes me pay
I'll show her something
one of these days
She makes me starve
She makes me blind
She makes me think I have no mind
I need her
I hate her
I want her
I love her
She looks good
And so does she

I know all of them want me
God damn, I'm a terminal man

I am a terminal woman
That last man felt like the last man
Just like the last time
Just like the last crime
I don't know how he does it
but he does
He does it over and over
The last time felt like the last time
and the time before

Every time I tell myself,
no more, no more
Every time I get knocked down
I crawl back
Why am I being punished
Why does love blacken my eyes
Split my lips and crack my ribs
Is he the right man
Is he the wrong man
Or is he just the man I need right now

LA Pain Central

Looking for an angel

Looking for a friend

Slipping into madness

A decline that never ends

Casting lies into tomorrow

Living yesterday's lies today

After all that you were given

How could you throw it all away?

Walking dazed and crooked

In a world of straight white lies

Telling me what my problem is

And telling me that

you're doing fine

Searching for a connection

Or something you can use

You think that people

are ladder rungs

I think you've got it all confused

You tell me that you're tired

But you never get to sleep

Do you think it's insomnia

Or the hours that you keep?

How can you take

Living in so much pain?

How can you take

Living in LA?

Untitled

Through waters unmuddied

I find you

I rise up from the depths

to find you here

My eyes are open

My vision is clear

For years I searched for you

When I stopped

I found you here

Don't make me

Make my body

Tell you a lie

Soul brother number none

Don't brother me

There's not another one

The mask is intact

I can't turn back

The face you see

Is all you'll see

I'm living and lying

Breathing and dying

Behind the mask

Unaffected, undetected

The surface is smooth

I make motionless moves

Behind the mask

The mask is cracking

The truth is coming out

Dirt and tears are falling through

Violence In The Street

(sung to the tune of

Dancing in the Street)

There'll be people slaying

Stray bullets spraying

A chance for Crips and Bloods

to bleed

There'll random killing

And real blood spilling

LAPD hours away

   It doesn't matter who you are

   Just as long as you don't care

   Everybody, in the 'hood

   Lock and load, it's understood

   There'll be violence

   Violence in the streets

There'll be bodies falling

Armageddon calling

And pre-teens dealing crack

There'll be bullets flying

And people dying

A chance to smoke some PCP

Down in South Central

Violence in the street

And in old Long Beach

Violence in the street

On the streets of Crenshaw

Violence in the street

But not in Belair

No violence in the street

Dig the snot

1989
Via Dolorosa

Your teeth are filed to points
You put ice into my joints

You stuff rocks into my shoes
You lose me in your blues

I tear myself apart
As I walk the dark roads of your heart
As lonely as I'll ever be
I know you'll always be there for me

Looking for a way to get away from you
I find myself 1000 miles further
down your throat

You are my howling desert
You are my stinging rain
You are the road I walk upon
And feel life's singing pain

With your iron fisted kindness
Shine your black light down on me
I'm staggering in my blindness
I need your eyes to see

Via Dolorosa
Can I stay with you awhile
I've walked the streets
of your crooked back
Just to see you smile

WORKING NOTES: The rock god walked out in front of adoring thousands night after night. They applauded everything he did. The adoring masses had no idea that he had been throwing up in his hotel room right up to an hour before show time. They roared approval when he was so smacked out he could barely speak and just moaned and laughed. Onstage he could do no wrong, not even when he tried. It was like a curse. All he could do offstage was destroy himself. Night after night. Some days he was unable to get up and plane reservations had to be canceled and rescheduled, because he, the great one, had ruined himself again the night before. To many he was a hero, a god. To others he was an enigma. To others still he was a manipulative coward who craved constant attention. They all expected to him to die, and why not, only geniuses can die young. They made him think he was beyond life. He was pathetic, sad, lost. He took a lot of people with him.

Sim sings "The Ditmar Song," Vienna, Austria, 1989

Paradise Found/
Paradise Lost

Paradise Found

This sheltering sky

The warmth around me

Your beautiful words and

how they lie

Your beautiful eyes and how they

burn holes into me

That I can't see

That I can't feel

Your beautiful face,

this beautiful place

My pain has left me

The bloodstain on my shirt grows

It is the warmth that I feel

Your embrace – Paradise

How you attract addict

and annihilate

With such perfection

You destroy me

Paradise Lost

Shipwrecked cornered traitor

ugly lover

Everything's moving,

dismantling, leaping apart

What have I done, where am I,

Where can I go

I can't see how easily I took

and took for granted

If you could have seen what I saw

Felt what I felt

You would know the pain of

losing what I lost

I know how Eternity feels right now

NOTES: I was in Berlin on a speaking tour. Beate from the band Matador asked me if I wanted to be on one of the songs on their upcoming album. Their first LP "A Touch Beyond Canned Love" was one of my favorite records of 1987. I said yes. She said that the song was called "Paradise" and the group wanted to do a Miltonesque thing, you know, Paradise Lost-Paradise Found. I could do whatever I wanted, they would sample my voice into the song. A few nights later I read this thing into my tape recorder and sent her the tape. Several months later I got a CD of the Matador album "Sun."

CHAPTER 6 - WARTIME

CHAPTER 6: WARTIME

Henry, Andrew

WARTIME

It was 1986. I was in the back of the van. Andrew Weiss, the bass player in the opening band Gone was talking about his small home studio he had named War Time Studios because the whole thing was hanging together on the extreme cheap. He was talking about how great it would be if there was some Go-Go music (a style of music that is indigenous to the Washington DC area, made legendary by such bands as Trouble Funk, Chuck Brown and the Soul Searchers, Experience Unlimited, Rare Essence, etc.) that had a harder edge. I had been thinking along the same lines for a long time. I said that we should form a band and call it War Time after his studio and do some hard-core go-go jams. It's the kind of thing you talk about on long drives to gigs. ✶✶✶

By the summer of 1987, Andrew and I were playing together. We had some time off between tours so we started the War Time project. We made a demo of the song War Time and a version of the Grateful Dead's Franklin's Tower. We played the demo to people and they were impressed. Our friend Kate Hyman at Chrysalis Records heard it and got us a small deal for an EP and there we were, our little idea had a home. We were on Chrysalis for a moment. It was what Mike Watt calls, "A bend in the road."

We recorded on and off through 1988 and eventually it was done. Andrew produced and Theo engineered. The record came out and we did a video for the song Truth. Jesse Dylan, son of the great Bob, directed.

I think the record has long been out of print. It was a valiant effort nonetheless and it was great to see something through from a concept to actually holding the record in your hand.

Here are the lyrics written for the project. Some were used, some not.

War Time

So little time, so much to deal
with. It seems that everything
Passes me on, turns me off, messes
me up, or just plain bums me out.
I crack my head when I try to get
over. I stub my toes when I try to
pass under. My existence is like to
breathe in a big rock. I inhale and
it hits me hard. I pay guys with
guns to protect me from guys with
guns. Some man in a suit is telling
me to drop dead so I can live
happily ever after. There's a guy in
the mirror who's always in my face.
Sometimes I think I'm going insane.

Don't lose your mind when you're
running through the mind field
Don't stop driving when you're
rolling on the real wheel
You've got to look the lie right in
the eye
And not be afraid to see too clearly
Makes no difference if it's night or day
I can take a look around and say
It's war time

That's what I'm talking about man,
that is exactly what I'm talking
about. The most important thing is
to maintain. Sometimes it's all you
can do not to want to take a gun
and put it right to your brain.
Sometimes it's all you can do just
to maintain. Looking out on the
streets, seeing those human rats
racing. Running wild like mindless
idiots will run wild. I can't
believe the groove they choose.
Tearless eyes cry, fearless eyes
lie. Talking about change so they
can remain the same: shameless
nameless and free from blame. It's
enough to make you want to do

something down right stupid. It's enough to make you do something down right sick.

Stand back so you can laugh at the negative fools who met their match. They can't find the time to find their minds so they run a vicious circle till the day they die. They blew it, don't do it. I'm amazed at the maze, people lost in a haze. I see them standing in line for the rest of their days. Never question the boss, might get thrown for a loss. Obey? Ok, but how much will it cost? Can't pay the rent all your money's been spent on that coke what a joke. Your watch is in hock since the stock market fell straight to hell and you fell to your knees from the force of the shock oh well. Searching your mind for the answer in time to escape from the rape of a system so blind. Your heroes show zeros, they're burning like Nero, up in the flames of the games that they played. Questions no answers, it kills you like cancer and all of a sudden you can't keep the pace. Living for money and isn't it funny how something like hope can blow up in your face?

These days I run into a lot of negative folks running all backwards out of the mouth and to them I say: This groove deals with a place called right here and a time called right now. Now if you're not here then you're somewhere else and that's nowhere so I guess that you don't care. Now you can try to deny it and lie, and it's a shame that you're so lame that you don't have the guts to stand up. This thing is righteous, outrageous and conta- gious. This deal appeals to muta- tions manifestations and deviations of all persuasions. This is an all seeing, all knowing, ever flowing unrestrained uncontained force of nature and it will not be falsified, classified and put on the shelf to start a major league dust collec- tion. This is a constitutional above board on the level freak out. So let's kick it.

So now you know what the deal is. The time is war time. War time is here, it's all around you. You can't close your eyes and make it go away. To be alive right here, right now, right here in the here and now is to be dealing with a 24 hour a day, 360 degree war time reality. It's a full time thing, you got to deal with it. You hang on you'll be alright.

You've go to keep moving in a
positive forward direction. If you
let them they will destroy you.
Don't let them. Say to yourself:
They will not destroy me, they will
not destroy me.

WORKING NOTES: I turn the streets clean with the
power of my vision. I can turn a pile of garbage into a
mountain of roses. All I have to is maintain. It gets so hard
to maintain. I keep seeing the great airstrike burning every
thing clean. If they're going to act dead we might as well
give them the other half of the deal. If you don't see it then
you've been had. If you say that everything's fine then you
got the disease. When you say it's not there then it's bigger
than you could possibly imagine. Modern man grew eyes in
the back of his head of keep up with the 9mm pace of the
world. Someday it will all be one or the other--Jungle or Desert.

Life
I've got endless frustration
It seems like there's no end
It's as if I am alive to serve
and be thankful
Humbled and intimidated, humiliated
daily, shoved and folded
Reduced to a self-pitying heap
of worshipping flesh
Shove your monument to
misery and strife
Right up your psychosis

I see your poison dream
I know just what it means
It won't work for me
You're not what you seem
I see right through your screen

You can't make me bleed
Oh you lie
And you try
I don't buy
I resist
And you twist
You persist

Take a look around at the hate game
that they're playing
Look at the guilt trip that
they're laying on you
Don't think that this is the
dawn of the pawn
Don't think that you're the
first to be put upon
The only one that came undone
In the shortcomings of the long run
It's not like that,
strike that non-fact
Leave the suckers for the clowns
Take a look around

You must think I'm blind
Born without a mind
It's time to rise and shine
Criminal 9 to 5
It takes up all your time
It's time to see the light
Heartless mindless fools
Use people just like tools
I'm not a human mule

Beat down human blues
Paying endless dues

I've got the real news

Criminality's your specialty
Going to the head of the class
Right off the top you do the rip-off
Like you're some kind of scholar
Running rings around the dollar
When the cash is running you ragged
into the bag
Until your eyes are trying to exit
through the back of your head
Six feet into the ground
Take a look around

Put this on the map
I'm not going out like that
I'll tell you where it's at
Truth is what I use
The same thing you abuse
I've got the mind to choose
Here I am
In your face
Right now is the place
It's so hard to be free
Means everything to me
Use your eyes to see

Take A Look Around

Take a look around at the sight
that confines you
Take a look around as it seeks
to define you
Try to find a way to keep
your head above the heads above

Take a look around as
the crime rate rises
Hear the sad sad story of a
date rape crisis
Glad for the day that holds
no surprises
No news is good news now go on home
and sing the blues
Look for a reason to keep on
keeping at it

Take a look around at the hatred
that burns
Like a fuse of abuse as the
pages get turned
Take a look around as the lesson
gets learned
Time is laughing, time is
killing us slow
You can see the fear
everywhere you go

Take a look around do you
like what you see
Can you look me in the eye
and tell me you're free
Do you know the difference between
who you are
And what they want you to be
I'm fed up, it's either get up and
load up or get the hell out

Take a look around as
the lean get leaner
Crawling like bugs as

the weak get meaner
Over the hill and off
to heaven they go

Take a look around at
the grind that finds you
Down in the hole with your life
behind you
Looking for a friend to tell you
it's going to be alright

Take a look around at the
a war that's fought
Where cars drive by and
bullets get shot
And killers get caught by
killers who have the right

Take a look around can you separate
yourself
From that which tries to separate
you from yourself
It's hard to stay one and
not become one too

Take a look around put
yourself in the mirror
See the one who sees you clearer
Realize the terror of
the error of the era
As it puts you in the place where
your face gets chased
Half way off your head
This dream, this madness,

this drastic gladness
All the while you get the
air-conditioned unconditional smile
My decision: no submission
On my mission, listen to the sound,
take a look around
Better to create a solution than to
perpetuate this lying illusion
Reality has a way of doing it to you
Real is real as real can be

Big Trouble

Hacking through the red tape home to
the yellow tape blues
Dead teenagers turning up on
the evening news
See yourself dwarfed when
you see the big picture
Feel the fear as
the picture gets clearer

Sitting alone hoping that
the phone will start ringing
Knowing that the sound of sirens
can't be angels singing
Somewhere someone out there
is getting done up – unfair
But all the same it's not you –
this time

High tension mounting on the subway
No sidelong glances not taking any
chances no way

Hand on the briefcase running for
the staircase
Strangulation collar sweating hard
for the dollar
Big trouble

Riding high on a lie
Looking through an evil eye for
someone to blame
Come down from your tower to find
that it's all the same
When you look into the mirror a
troubled man appears
Don't freak out when
your reason for living
Becomes your reason to live in fear

Some people are getting
hostile down right mad
They say they've got a right
to be and it makes me sad
Walking wounded by anger
Running blinded by rage
Go to sleep in your bed
wake up in their cage
Go figure
Big trouble

You want trouble
More than you've already got?
Well then step right up
And get some of this
trouble that's hot
You came to the right place if

you're looking for trouble
Because trouble is all
that we've got

Not Going Out Like That

I see a world that seeks
to destroy me
Neutralize harness and employ me
Suckers and thieves want a piece of
my mind no way
I've got an out I'm not a victim
of authority
I've still got my mind that
makes me the minority
I've got one fact:
I'm not going out like that
Racists, I've got a problem with you
And your plans to destroy those who
are different than you
I'll be exact and keep my
statement intact:
I'm not going out like that
Terrified hands shaking
Reaching out for a friend
Looking hard, can't see the enemy
Look again
It might be you not me
Can't you see, they're taking you
to the end
Take the blinders off your eyes
and look again
I'm not going out like that

CHAPTER 7 - 1990-1992

1990

In 1990 we wrote songs and played eighty-one shows. When off the road, we were centered in Trenton, NJ. Sim's mother Audrey generously allowed Chris and I to sleep in her front room. During this time we would go almost daily to Andrew's house in Hopewell, NJ and work on songs.

By the end of 1990, we had a pretty strong set of music. It was a hard won batch of tunes. Sim was the only one with a car so he had to drive us to practice every day. Andrew had to have a bunch of band types at his place several days a week and that added stress to the mix. Also, we all butted heads in the songwriting process. Your basic band stuff but in a cold basement on no income, it can get intense. Our heat source was a kerosene heater and after awhile, the fumes would get to you. Good music often comes from a tense environment, although it often takes a toll on the players. In art, anything good comes with a price. ✶ ✶ ✶

Low Self Opinion

I think you got a
low self opinion man
I see you standing all by yourself
Unable to express
The pain of your distress
You withdraw deeper inside
You alienate yourself
And everybody else
They wonder what's on your mind
They got so tired of you
And your self-ridicule
They wrote you off and
left you behind

You sleep alone at night
You never wonder why
So much bitterness wells up
inside you
You always victimize
So you can criticize yourself
And all those around you

The hatred you project
Does nothing to protect you
You leave yourself so exposed
You want to open up
When someone says
Hey, lighten up
You find all your doors closed
Get yourself a break from
self-rejection

Try some introspection
And you just might find
It's not so bad and anyway
At the end of the day
All you have is yourself
and your mind

You've got a low self opinion
I see how it breaks you down
I see how it messes you around

The self hatred that blinds you
Binds you grinds you keeps you down
The world falls down around you
You build up walls around you
You wear disgust like a crown

If you could see the you that I see
When I see you seeing me
You'd see yourself so differently
Believe me

I know the self doubt that runs
inside your mind
I know the self doubt that treats
you so unkind

If you could see the you that I see
When I see you
You would see things differently
I assure you

Ladies and Gentlemen . . . Sim Cain

WORKING NOTES: He had it wired, he could protect himself by shielding himself with his own hatred. He would never have to try, any failure would be a success. Maintaining his low self-esteem became his way to pass the time. He didn't have to look far, there was always someone around to make him feel like a fool. Sometimes he helped. He came to need fuel to keep it going.

VERSE I   LOW S-O

PAGE NO.

PREPARED BY
DATE

OFFENSIVE
DEFENSIVE

1 I THINK YOU GOT A LOW SELF OPINION
2 I SEE YOU STANDING ALL BY YOURSELF
3 UNABLE TO EXPRESS
4 THE PAIN OF YOUR DISTRESS
5 YOU WITHDRAW DEEPER INSIDE
6 YOU ALIENATE YOURSELF
7 AND EVERYBODY ELSE
8 THEY WONDER WHATS ON YOUR MIND YOUR MINDS
9 YOU SPEND SO MUCH TIME
10 PUTTING EVERYTHING DOWN   I THINK YOU GOT
11 THAT THEY WROTE YOU OFF AND LEFT   LOW S/O O'S
12 X AND LEFT YOU BEHIND   YOUR SELF HATRED'S
13   WHAT BLINDS YOU
14 THEY GOT TIRED OF YOU / AND ALL Y. RIDICULE BINDS GRINDS YOU
15 THEY WROTE YOU OFF   KEEPS YOU DOWN
16 AND LEFT YOU BEHIND   YOU SAY THAT YOU DONT CARE
                                      AND THAT YOU'RE GOING NO WHERE
17   YOU'VE GOT NO
18   THE WORLD FALLS   FRIENDS AROUND
19   DOWN AROUND YOU   YOU PULL YOUR   WHY DO YOU WONDER
20   YOU PUT UP   WHY
21   WALLS AROUND
22   YOU / YOU   WEAR SELF DISGUST   MISTRUST
23   LIKE A CROWN   SELF DISGUST
24   SELF CONTEMPT
25
26
27
28 executive

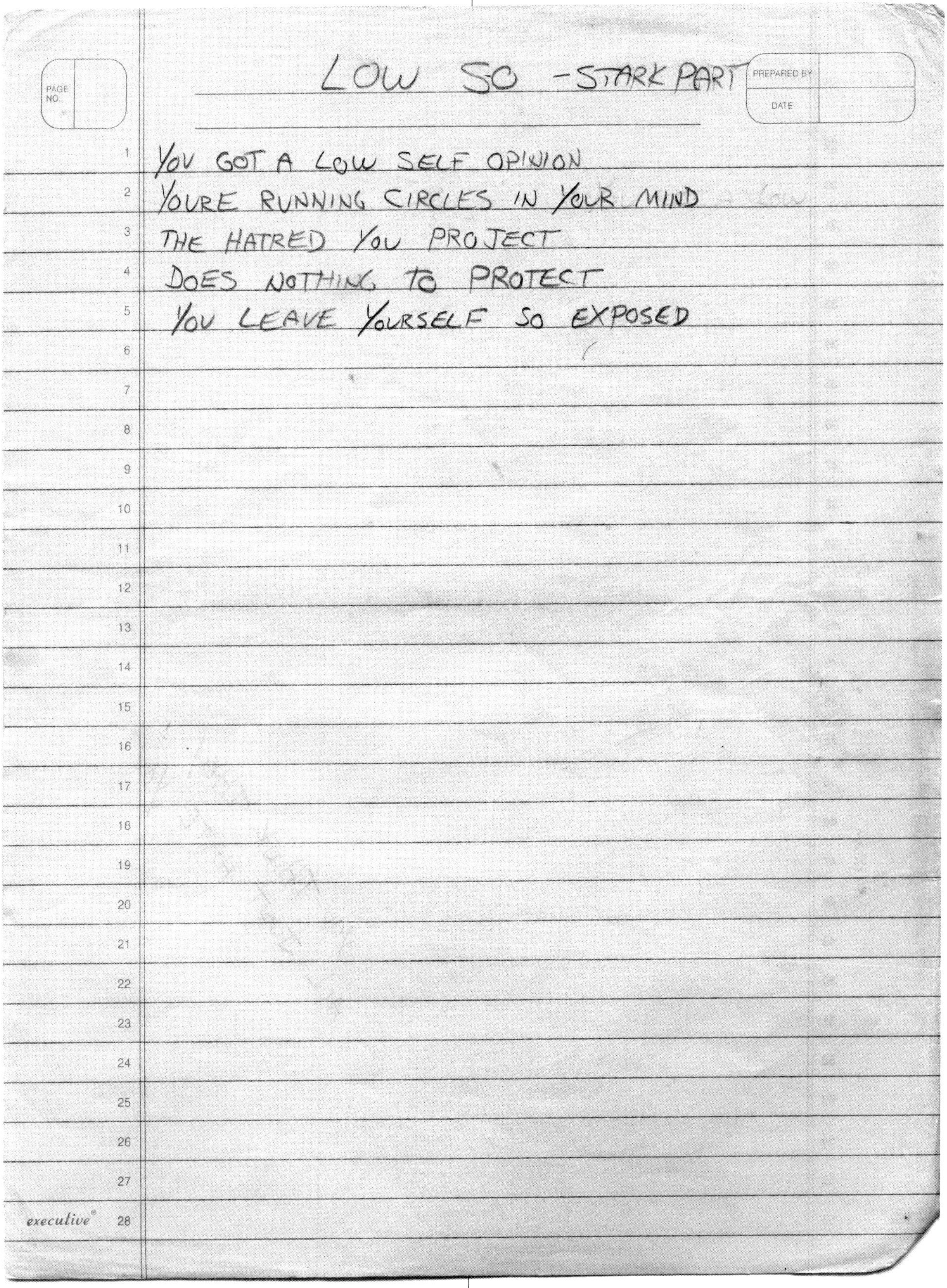

LOW SO -STARK PART

PREPARED BY

DATE

PAGE NO.

1 YOU GOT A LOW SELF OPINION
2 YOU'RE RUNNING CIRCLES IN YOUR MIND
3 THE HATRED YOU PROJECT
4 DOES NOTHING TO PROTECT
5 YOU LEAVE YOURSELF SO EXPOSED

executive

PAGE NO.

YOUR MIND

BURN/LEARN

PREPARED BY

DATE

YOU SLEEP ALONE AT NIGHT
~~HATE EVERYTHING THATS IN YOUR SIGHT~~
YOU NEVER WONDER WHY
SO MUCH BITTERNESS WELLS UP INSIDE YOU
YOU ALWAYS VICTIMIZE
TO HELP YOU CRITCIZE
YOURSELF AND ~~THOSE~~ AROUND YOU

SO ALONE
NO REASON
WHY
EXCEPT YOU

YOUVE

IF YOU COULD SEE THE YOU THAT I SEE
YOU MIGHT SEE YOURSELF SO DIFFERENTLY

YOU JUST MIGHT SEE YOURSELF

ecutive®

UNWELCOMED SONGS

Chris

Human

If I kill you then you die
If you kill me then I die
When we die we die that's it
Until then you're human don't quit

This life steps in unexplained
Smiles and stares as you burn in
flames
Turns to go and says
Serves you right
Leaves you cold and so uptight
Leaves you crawling blind with need

Makes you bite the hand that feeds
Grabs and drags you by your heels
And makes you feel like
a human feels

Build a monument with your emotions
Destroy it with the tangled world
of your illusion
Destroy yourself with the way it
ought to be
Lose yourself forever
In someone else's version
of your reality

Who told you
There was more to life than this?
Who told you there was more to life
than life itself?
When we crumble
When we fall
You'll see there was no truth at all
Just the mind games that we played
Just the choices that we made

WORKING NOTES: Is there a life after this one? Let me read your palm. What's your sign? You're born. You feed it, you sleep it. You find creative ways to poison and endanger it so you can feel more aware of its presence. Finally it gives out and you die. I'm not impressed with crystals around the neck. It makes you feel better about the fact that you're going to die. So fuck it, keep destroying until it gives out. At least you went for it. It's all blood and bones. If a pig shoots you, if you shoot yourself...when you die you're dead. Until then you're on the way. Every second that passes by is one second closer to the last one. Take hold and make it all count, or make none of it count, when it's over, it's over all the way. When you're eighty and sitting on the front porch you'll wish you did.

PRODUCTION NOTE: This song made it as far as the 2.11.91 demo. The last time it was played live was in Manchester UK 5.30.91. It was then dropped.

Andrew, Theo

Obscene

I'm so confused
Can't find the line
Between what I use and abuse

So unreal
How I lie and try to deny
The things that I feel

I'll love you and hate you both at
the same time
Heal you and hurt you and
laugh as you cry

Why I don't know
Right at you right in you
Right through you right past you
I go

Can't you see
First it's him then it's her
Then it's us then it's you
Then it's me

Depression elation and heartbreak
all mine
Refinement confinement all my design

You and me
Pathetic we cling
We think that we're free

Ugly
You and me
You see, you see the real me

So obscene
Flapping wildly
You see what I mean

Keep away
Can't see why you do what you do
And say what you say

WORKING NOTES: Get close and see it, face it. It's ugly. Life isn't beautiful, it's obscene. What you'll do for a fuck, what you'll do to be happy. You'd swallow dirt if you thought it would make it any easier for you. No one escapes the beating. Violence is the expression of pure survival. Life is violence. You're attracted to it. There's nothing you can do to tell me that it doesn't draw you like a moth to flame, sucker. Humans can't help themselves, they know too much, it will be the crippling plague that kills us all. Good. I can't help but hurt you.

MO' EVIL / EVIL

RIFF MIGHT WORK IN HERE   I LOVE & HATE RIGHT NOW

CHORUS'S

I'M SO CONFUSED
CAN'T FIND THE LINE BETWEEN
WHAT I USE AND (WHAT I) ABUSE

STUPIDITY RISING MY ANGER IS BLINDING
~~BY~~ MY LOVE/~~HATE~~ HATE IS ALL THAT I SEE

STRICKEN AND SLAPPED   BITTEN & BRANDED
STUNG AL FLUNG INTO FIRE
I'M BURNING I'M BURNT

UGLY. YES. YOU AND ME.
IN FEAR WE CLING.
PATHETIC, WE THINK THAT WE'RE FREE

CAN'T YOU ~~SEE~~. FIRST ITS HIM THEN ITS
HER THEN ITS US THEN ~~●~~ ITS YOU THEN ITS ME

SO UNREAL   WE LIE ~~& TRY TO~~ AND HIDE & DENY
~~DENY~~ THE THINGS THAT WE FEEL

~~PLEASE~~ KEEP AWAY
CAN'T SEE WHY YOU DO WHAT DO
AND SAY THE THINGS THAT YOU SAY

WHY I DON'T KNOW RIGHT AT YOU
IN YOU, THRU YOU   RIGHT PAST YOU - GO

~~MINE~~
/MISERY (DEPRESSION'
ELATION AND
HEARTBREAK ALL MINE

REFINEMENT
CONFINEMENT
ALL MY DESIGN

I'LL LOVE YOU   AND HATE
YOU BOTH AT THE SAME TIME
HEAL YOU AND HURT YOU
AND LAUGH AS YOU CRY

Just Like You

I am the man in a human choke hold
I am a product of your restraint
I watched the years pass by me
Never once did I complain
Never once did I say no
Now I watch myself explode
My body is scarred by age
Now you get to taste my rage

From the wreckage of humiliation
I got my self-respect
I got myself together
What the hell did you expect?

You should feel the pain
I go through
When I see myself I see you
Everything that you did I do
When I see myself I see you
Rage

I'm just like you
My flesh isn't my flesh
My blood isn't my blood
I'm just like you
There's nothing I can do

Another Life

You must think you're
going to live forever
I listen to the lies as they fall
from your face
You must think that you are
mighty clever
Can't you find a better way to deal
with this place?

Watching your life die
You're watching your life die
We're all watching your life die
Your hands are wet
Your mouth is dry
You shake and sweat
You want to die
Your eyes are hot

Your skin is cold
You're so young
But you look so old

Lie in bed all day
staring at the ceiling
Your friends come around
Because they wonder
how you're feeling
You send them all away
Because you can't identify
They don't know you
They're not even high
So high
If I could make wishes come true
I know what I'd wish for you
Another life
Another life for you

WORKING NOTES: See the monkey's eyes. Look deep into the monkey's eyes as he comes to you smiling. Day after day the monkey's eyes become bigger and bigger. Soon the monkey's eyes are all you can see. Soon the monkey's eyes become your eyes. You feel the monkey's bite. Monkey see monkey do, monkey will destroy you.

Another one I know dies in his room alone, they find his body a few days later and all anyone can say is, "What a stupid motherfucker." He was one of the first people I met when I came out to LA. Now he's dead. Last time I saw him, he was at a Mexican restaurant on Rose and Lincoln. Always the same. A girl with him, talking shit about some band he had going. It took a few days for the pain to sink in. I think of his dead body and all the life that he will miss.

She is a student at one of the finest schools in the country, she's smart and should do well. That is when she doesn't have to miss class because she's out looking for smack. No one can tell her a damn thing, it's as if no one in the world has ever thought they knew exactly what they were doing and still got it wrong enough to wind up dead. She knows what she's doing, she can quit any time she wants so why don't you go fuck off and mind your own business and look the other way when she pukes on her pillow?

You're so high, you don't even matter. Life is hard, the hardest one there is. You want to get out all the time. Pick up a paintbrush, a pen, a camera, a phone, a guitar-- anything but a needle.

Blues Jam

```
They always pry
They always want to know why
Then they pull you close
They make you want to die


You never felt so good
You never felt so well understood
So then you open your heart right up
And say come on in
And then you'll find you're bleeding
And falling down again
```

Grip

See me
Put yourself in my place
Be me
Put my eyes in your face
Maybe then you'll see why this place
terrifies me
And why I have to get myself away
So hard to deal with the ones who
can't feel
They continually blow my mind

No need
I've been burned enough times myself
You're like me
Sometimes you scare yourself
The things that you think
And the way that you feel
Makes you think you're on your own
When you go outside
And try to find a familiar mind
It really lets you know
you're on your own
So unknown

When those walls close in around you
When all about you doubt you
When the world can live without you
Get a grip and keep it
You see how hard they'll shove you
Hate your guts and tell you

they love you
Get a grip right now
You see how far you get pushed
How long they'll hold you down
Feed you lies
Drive you insane
Give you poison to kill your pain

Know me
I see the fear in your eyes
Pull back
There are some things to realize

So hard to deal with the ones who
aren't real
It's unbelievable what
they'll put you through
Twist you up inside
Filthify and punish your mind
You don't have to live like that

You've got to get your self-respect
You've got to jump back
Keep your self-respect intact
You've got to keep it like that
Your self-respect

Almost Real

I looked deep into your eyes
Saw men lying broken
Shattered at the bottom of your well
You took their simple affection
Turned it into bad infection
Sent them packing straight to hell
I know what sweats you
Reality threatens you
You can't hide yourself from me
When you see the one that sees
through you - It's me

Canine men
Fighting, lying,
trying to be the one
That gets to feel your touch
I see them lined up like broken heroes
Spitting out pieces of their broken luck

I guess I've got good sense
and hindsight
Because to me it never meant
that much
When you see the one who laughs
at you - It's me

Wasted time spent thinking about you
You know I've come to hate myself
Smashing my hands against the wall
Trying to forget the foolish way
I felt
You're so kind when
it serves you well
Your cruelty

No more trying
No more lying
I'm tired of wasting my time

with games

I'm going, I'm gone

Because now I see you

You must think I'm blind

When you need those arms around you

You won't find my arms around you

When you see the one who sees

through you

When you see the one who laughs at

you - It's me

WORKING NOTES: I wish you just lied the whole time, then I would have known what to do. I feel stupid now. You're good though, you mixed enough truth to the lies that I fell for the whole thing, I believed it all, every damn thing that came out of your mouth. Almost real, that's what

you are. I don't know what makes you do what you do. I asked around about you, seems like you have done this to a few people as well. That one guy, apparently you really did a number on his head. You make people into suckers when they believe you. You turn them into heartbroken messes. You're a walking talking waste of time, I wish there was some way I could run up ahead and warn the others that will eventually fall into your drama.

"Essentially, cruelty means strictness, diligence and implacable resolution, irreversible and absolute determination. Cruelty is above all lucid, a sort of rigorous discipline, submission to necessity." - A. Artaud

WHOOPS: There's a line in this song, "Spitting out pieces of their broken luck." I thought it was a pretty good line. You bet it's good. It's one word different than a line from a Jethro Tull song called "Aqualung." I've had that record since I was fourteen. It never occurred to me until a critic pointed it out. Oh man! At least these pieces of shit are good for something. Anyway, my apologies to Ian Anderson and his fine line that I inadvertently ripped off.

Carry Me Down

Sweating and out of breath
Trying to regain your composure
You're that much closer to death
And you're freaking out from
the exposure
They get right under your skin
And get you running wild
And when you finally break down
They treat you like a child

Belligerent and full of shit
You're not getting any smarter
Everything makes you uptight
And life just seems to get harder

Trying so hard not to explode
Do what you can to maintain
There's nowhere you can go
And no one wants to listen to you
try to explain

Depression
Confession
Condition
Repetition
You're in deep

PRODUCTION NOTES: Ended up using this lyric on a session with the Hard-Ons, an Australian band. We recorded this at a radio station on a day off while on tour.

1991

1991 was a busy and eventful year. We played a lot of shows, were invited to go out on the first Lollapalooza tour and in the fall of that year we recorded The End of Silence album.

The shows were good and we were playing all the songs that were to be included on The End of Silence record so by the time we actually got into the studio, we would be ready.

Lollapalooza was one of the best times I have ever had on the road. We got to see the Butthole Surfers and Ice T every day, the food was good and then at the end of the night we got to go to a Jane's Addiction gig for free. I think that's about as good as it's going to get. I was sorry when the tour was over for two reasons: the tour was really great and the end of the tour meant the start of recording.

Recording was always somewhat difficult for one reason or another. I had a feeling that this time around it was going to be a special deluxe no-holds-barred pain-in-the-ass and much to my regret, I was right.

We went into a new studio called the Showplace in New Jersey. The Showplace is a large building, half studio, half strip bar. We used to play the strip bar part in the 80's. The studio was good and we got right to work with producer Andy Wallace.

Being the producer, Andy had ideas as to what the songs needed. Some of the ideas were used, others weren't. There was one point where he suggested we take off the beginning of the song Obscene and get right to the main riff. It was a

valid suggestion, what the hell. It was, however, the start of the divide between the band members and the producer.

A few days later, a Friday afternoon I think, we were gearing up for a good night of work when Andy announced he was going home and he'd see us on Monday. We looked at him like he was nuts, it's a Friday and we're ready to rock and he's treating this project like some job at a bank. That was the corner turned in the producer-band relationship. I even thought that was lame. Tensions started to mount. Members offered to leave the sessions. I was now in the position of being politician and band member. I'm in the room doing this, on the phone doing that and nothing seems to be good enough for some people and it occurred to me at this point in time that these people were never really going to be my friends, that they were the guys in the band and they would always see me as the boss, so why expend any extra energy trying to make it something that it wasn't? From that moment on, they were people I worked with. This was how it was all the way until we parted ways in 1997. Not to say I didn't love them dearly, but let's be realistic.

I learned a lot that fall. For a few years, we had been working with an agent in NYC who booked our shows well but when he came to see us play, he would never fail to remind us that he didn't like our music but didn't mind booking us. So strange that he actually showed surprise when I called him from the studio and told him that I was taking the band to a different agent who actually liked the band. In time, the agency I went to was swallowed up by a larger one who reinstated the apathy I had grown so used to. There's a lot of that in this business. Another lesson learned. No agent is ever going to be your friend. They book the shows and take their percentage and that's all you need to know.

After that experience I never brought any emotion to any relationship I have with anyone in the business world. I don't care what the fucking agent thinks of what we do. Book the damn shows and get out of my way. I don't care what the marketing guy at the label thinks of the music. Just market the fucking music and we'll go out and play it. It's why I leave almost nothing in the hands of record companies that is unfinished.

They get mastered and sequenced records, finished artwork, etc. For this I am called a control freak. Better this than someone who holds their record up and asks, "What the hell is this?" because they weren't there when that part of the record was being dealt with. I digress.

In any case, we finished work on the record quickly and soon it was all mixed and done with. All the members of the band had a problem with the record. There were complaints. I thought it was a pretty damn good record and came to the conclusion that I didn't give a fuck what they thought. So shut the fuck up and let's go on tour, if that's ok by you. You do tour, don't you? And go on tour we did.

Break

Start over

Break

Get up

Rise to the occasion

Break

Time takes time

Break it

Break it off

Freedom is here

So clear

Let go-break

Snap the spine

Shake off the fear

Shrug off the excess

Break

Snap it

Wrap it around a dead end

Time steals time

Break

Pull back

See it — see it all

Keep moving

Invent yourself

Inventory parental damage

This is it

Life begins with the first breath

Break or get broken

Break it up — don't break down

WORKING NOTES: Television trip wires funeral pyres backstage fires. No need. Life long hurdle. You passed the mark before you jumped and now you're flying and you don't know to where or why. Just break. I see mother's eyes flashing. Father fear is never too far away. So break, pull back and see yourself. You wonder what the rush is. Why

the fury and rage inside is so strong and persistent. Break. Take yourself higher. Your parent's shoes are made of lead. Their touch is polio. You run on gold and sunlight. Blood and steel. You forge beauty when you break.

Even

Fuck you

Thanks for letting me

watch those men

Fuck you

Go get killed

Thanks for filling me with

fear and rage

Go blow your brains out

Go fuck fuck fuck

Fuck yourself

Stop

Fucking me

Go rip your teeth out with pliers

Die so I can live

Don't forget to fuck

Fuck fuck fuck

Mutilate yourself

Stop mutilating me

Mother, you're not my mother

Father, you're not my father

Brother, I don't have a brother

I think I'll use you

I think I'll use

You

I think I'll turn around

And break you

I'll ruin your life

I'll damage ya good

Then we'll be even

Your Life

Pick through the brains

of civilization

Try to find enough space to

fit your dreams

Feel like a criminal when you get

what you want

Duck for cover as

the entire city screams

Run motherfucker run

Keep going until you get it right

That red light

That gun fight

All the statistics

Scare tactics

It's you

It's your life

The street opens in front of you

You see the terror

Watch life pass you by

Watch the dust fall from your eyes

This is real life

Your life

Rip it to shreds

Blow its brains out

Still it comes back to you

1992

We toured a lot of 1992. One hundred and sixty-five shows in all. We opened for the Chili Peppers, we opened for the Beastie Boys, we did our own shows. We played everywhere three times or something. The shows were good. Things became increasingly strained. The last show of the year was with the Beasties in San Francisco. That was our last show with Andrew the bass player. He quit and he was fired at the same time, take your pick, either one is fine with me as long as I don't have to play with the guy anymore.

Didn't write a lot of new music in this time. We were onstage most nights and in the small spaces of down time, I don't think anyone wanted to work on songs. A lot of jams with improvised words but nothing written down. That was one long year but the shows were damn good and that's all that matters.

A NOTE TO ALL BANDS: If you don't tour, if you can't do it without backing tape, if you can't deliver the goods live, then you're shit. For a band, the live show tells the complete truth. If you're not good enough, then work at it until you are. If you think the stage is a place to fuck around and waste people's time and degrade the almighty force that is music, then face the facts. It's a brand new day so let a man come in and do the popcorn.

SCATHE

I ERASE MYSELF IN FRONT OF YOU

IT IS MY FEAR THAT MAKES ME STRONG

IT IS MY KNOWLEDGE THAT I WOULD NOT SURVIVE THAT MAKES ME ACHELLE.

IT'S MY SELF-HATRED ~~THAT~~ HAS BROUGHT SMILES TO MANY

AND WHAT LOOKS TO YOU LIKE CONFIDENCE, IS NOTHING BUT A SHIELD OF ~~DENIAL~~ DESPERATION

MY ACCEPTANCE OF MY INADEQUACIES HAS SCARRED MY SKIN AND BROKEN MY BONES

WHAT YOU SEE IS ONE THING — WHAT I AM IS SOMETHING ELSE

IT'S MY DESIRE TO BE LIKE YOU THAT HAS ~~FORCED MY ME TO SURPASS YOU~~ INSTILLED ~~THE WITH~~ IN ME THE NEED TO SURPASS YOU ~~EVERY TIME~~ UNTIL ~~IT KILLS ME~~ I DIE

WEAK & UNWASHED THE WRETCHED

HENRY ROLLINS

UNWELCOMED SONGS

UNWELCOMED SONGS

HENRY ROLLINS

UNWELCOMED SONGS

HENRY ROLLINS

UNWELCOMED SONGS

TONIGHT'S PERFORMANCE

⑩

DOORS OPEN ___6:30___   KALAMAZOO

SHOW TIME ___8:00___

CREW MEAL ___5·30___

ARTIST PERFORMANCE TIMES

H.R.B. FROM __8:15__ TO __9:00__

SET CHANGE __1__ FROM __9:00__ TO __9:30__

STUART ROSS + JA. FROM __9:30__ TO __10:45.__

SET CHANGE _____ FROM _____ TO _____

_____ FROM _____ TO _____

Nice to have Henry Rollin's
on the Lollapalozza Festival

HENRY ROLLINS

HENRY ROLLINS

UNWELCOMED SONGS

© 1991 Keith Krishman

HENRY ROLLINS

HENRY ROLLINS

UNWELCOMED SONGS

アナタのための
ヘヴィ・メタル

THE END OF SILENCE

俺の夢はアメリカ中でテロをやることだった。
それが今や実現しつつあるってわけさ

LA暴動の真っ只中にいたヘンリー・ロリンズが語りまくる暗黒大陸アメリカ
問答無用、怒濤のヘヴィ・ロックを生み出したその背景とは？

インタビュー●大谷英之　協力●ブライアン・バートンルイス／田村亜紀

溜まりに溜まったフラストレーションを一気に爆発させる。ハード・ロック、パンク、とロックの伝統的とも言えるそういった方法論はこれまでにも数多くあった。ヘンリー・ロリンズ率いるロリンズ・バンドの新作「エンド・オブ・サイレンス」もある意味で全く新しい音ではない。ファンクやラップを取り入れた等再構築という時代の胎動とは逆に、白人ロックの可能性を丹念に掘り下げた結果。で上がったのがこの漆黒大のヘヴィ・ロックである。

*この間はレッド・ホット・チリ・ペッパーズと一緒にツアーしてたんですよね。まずはその辺から聞かせてください。

PIC: TIBOR BOZU/LGI/IMPERIAL PRESS 37

PIC: STEVE JENNINGS/LGI/IMPERIAL PRESS 39

UNWELCOMED SONGS

HENRY ROLLINS

UNWELCOMED SONGS

HENRY ROLLINS

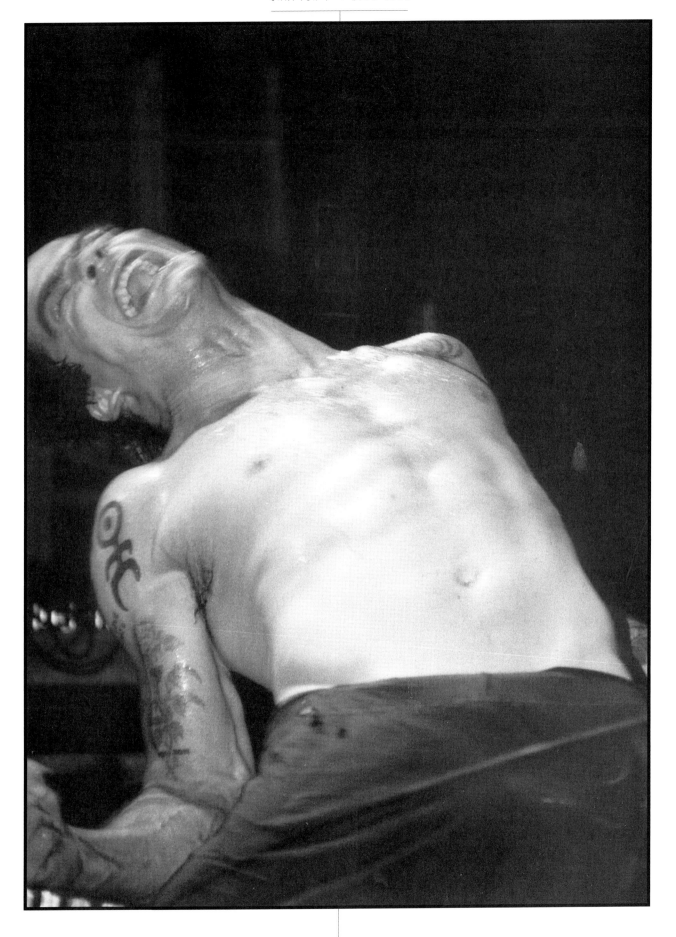

UNWELCOMED SONGS

HENRY ROLLINS

Australia 1990, Joe Cole on right with video camera

CREDITS

All lyrics by Henry Rollins.

All lyrics copyright 2.13.61, Inc.

Page 3:   Photo by Unknown.

Page 4:   Photo by Susie J.

Page 5:   Photo by Susie J.

Page 6:   Photo (top) by Ian MacKaye.

    Photo (bottom) by Susie J.

Page 9:   Photo by Susie J.

Page 12:   Photo by Susie J.

Page 13:   Photo (top) by Susie J.

    Photo (bottom) by Wanda Luciani.

Page 14:   Photo by A. Angelos.

Page 18:   Photo by Tiffany Pruitt.

Page 19:   Photo by Spot.

Page 20:   Photo (top) Spot.

    Photo (bottom) by Paul May.

Page 21:   Photo (top) by Paul May.

    Photo (bottom) by Unknown.

Page 22:   Photo (top) by Fer Youz.

    Photo (bottom) by Fer Youz.

Page 23:   Photo (top) by Tiffany Pruitt.

    Photo (bottom) by Tiffany Pruitt.

Page 24:   Photo by Dina Douglass.

Page 25:   Photos by Doug Diaz.

Page 26:   Photo by K. Salk.

Page 27:   Photo by Unknown.

Page 28:   Photo by Brian Maurer.

Page 29:   Photo by Mike Pearson.

Page 30:   Photo (top) by Naomi Petersen.

    Photo (bottom) by Mike Pearson.

Page 31:   Photo by Mike Pearson.

Page 32:   Photo by Robert Lindsay.

Page 33:   Photo (top) by Robert Lindsay.

    Photo (bottom) by Naomi Petersen.

Page 34:   Photo by Robbie Robinson.

Page 35:   Photo (top) by Greg Blair.

    Photo (bottom) by Unknown.

Page 36-37:   Photo by Klik Abstrakt.

Page 38-39:   Photo by Naomi Petersen.

Page 40-41:   Photo by Naomi Petersen.

Page 42:   Photos by Greg Blair.

Page 43:   Photo by Gene Ambo.

Page 46:   Photo by Chris Haskett.

Page 47:   Photo by Chris Haskett.

Page 53:   Photo by Chris Haskett.

Page 56:   Photo by Ken Salerno.

Page 57:   Photo by Suzan Carson.

Page 58:   Photo by Unknown.

Page 59:   Photos by Suzan Carson.

Page 60:   Photo by Unknown.

Page 61:   Photo by Ken Salerno.

Page 62:   Photos by Chris Haskett.

Page 63:   Photos by Chris Haskett.

Page 64:   Photo by Chris Haskett.

Page 65:   Photo by Chris Haskett.

Page 66:   Photo by Chris Haskett.

Page 67:   Photo (top) by Unknown.

           Photo (bottom) Chris Haskett.

Page 68:   Photo by Chris Haskett.

Page 69:   Photos by Chris Haskett.

Page 70:   Photo by Ken Salerno.

Page 71:   Photo by Ken Salerno.

Page 72:   Photo by Ken Salerno.

Page 73:   Photo by Ken Salerno.

Page 74:   Photo by Tibor Bozi.

Page 75:   Photo by Unknown.

Page 76:   Photo by Joe Cole.

Page 77:   Photo by Joe Cole.

Page 78:   Photos by Unknown.

Page 79:   Photo by Tibor Bozi.

Page 80:   Photo by Catherine Ceresole/Bachmann.

Page 86:   Photo by Yvonne Baumann.

Page 87:   Photo by Silvia Van Hijfte.

Page 88:   Photo (top) by Yvonne Baumann.

           Photo (bottom) by Unknown.

Page 89:   Photo by Zetenyi Zoltan.

Page 90:   Photo (top) by Sponge.

           Photo (bottom) by Zetenyi Zoltan.

Page 91:   Photo (top) by Unknown.

           Photo (bottom) by Sponge.

Page 92:   Photo by Unknown.

Page 93:   Photo by Yvonne Baumann.

Page 94:   Photos by Unknown.

Page 95:   Photo by Rene Vanes.

Page 96:   Photo (top) by John Halfhide.

           Photo (bottom) by Unknown.

Page 97:   Photo by Unknown.

Page 98:   Photo (top) by Silvia Van Hijfte.

           Photo (bottom) by Unknown.

Page 99:   Photos by Sponge.

Page 100:   Photo by Zetenyi Zoltan.

Page 101:   Photo by Unknown.

Page 102:   Photos by Unknown.

Page 103:   Photo by Yvonne Baumann.

Page 104:   Photos by Unknown.

Page 105:   Photo by Unknown.

Page 106:   Photo by Unknown.

Page 107:   Photo by Ken Salerno.

Page 108:   Photo by Unknown.

Page 109:   Photo by Remco.

Page 110:   Photo by Unknown.

Page 111:   Photo by Unknown.

Page 112:   Photo by Yvonne Baumann.

Page 113:   Photo by Ken Salerno.

Page 114:   Photo by Unknown.

Page 115:   Photo by Unknown.

Page 116:   Photo by Yvonne Baumann.

Page 118:   Photo by Unknown.

Page 120:   Photo by Nicole Van Putte.

Page 123:   Photo by Shawn Scallen.

Page 124:   Photo by Roger Nufei.

Page 126:   Photo by Rene Vanes.

Page 127:   Photo by Unknown.

Page 128:   Photo by Hirko.

Page 132:   Photo by Michael Lavine.

Page 133:   Photo by Michael Lavine.

Page 142:   Photo by Andy Booth.

Page 143:   Photo by Steven Messina.

Page 145:   Photo by Chris Haskett.

Page 149:   Photo by S. Malzkorn.

Page 150:   Photo by Unknown.

Page 151:   Photo by Chris Haskett.

Page 154:   Photo by Chris Haskett.

Page 155:   Photo by Chris Haskett.

Page 156:   Photo by Chris Haskett.

Page 157:   Photo by Chris Haskett.

Page 159:   Photo by Chris Haskett.

Page 160:   Photo by Chris Haskett.

Page 161:   Photo by Chris Haskett.

Page 162:   Photo by Unknown.

Page 164:   Photo by Mick Geyer.

Page 166:   Photo by Unknown.

Page 167:   Photo by Unknown.

Page 169:   Photo by S. Malzkorn.

Page 170:   Photos (top row) by Unknown.

Photo (bottom row left) by Buffie Bogue.

Photo (bottom row right) by Unknown.

Page 171:   Photo by Karen Clements.

Page 172:   Photo by Unknown.

Page 173:   Photos (top left & top right upper)

by Jim Altieri.

Photo (top right lower) by Lisa Gourley.

Photo (bottom) by Unknown.

Page 174:   Photos by Unknown.

Page 175:   Photo by Unknown.

Page 176:   Photo by Unknown.

Page 177:   Photos by Unknown.

Page 178:   Photo (top row right) by Ciaffardini.

Photo (bottom row left) by Unknown.

Photo (bottom row rt.) by Chrissy Piper

Page 179:   Photo by Unknown.

Page 180:   Photo by Owen Sweeney.

Page 181:   Photos by Unknown.

Page 182:   Photos (top row) by Unknown.

Photo (bottom left) by Andy Booth.

Photo (bottom right) by Buffie Bogue.

Page 183:   Photo by Dave Tufts.

Page 184:   Photo by Keith Hershman

Page 185:   Photo (top) by Imagery.

Photo (bottom) by Unknown.

Page 186:   Photos by Karen Clements.

Page 187:   Photo by Karen Clements.

Page 188:   Photos by Unknown.

Page 189:   Photo by Lisa Gourley.

Page 190:   Photo by S. Malzkorn.

Page 191:   Photo by S. Malzkorn.

Page 192:   Photos by Unknown.

Page 193:   Photo by Rene Vanes.

Page 194:   Photo by Zoe.

Page 195:   Photo (upper left)

by Jorn Gerrit Steinmann.

Photo (upper right) by Andy Booth.

Photo (bottom) by Mick Geyer.